INTERNET POLICIES AND ISSUES

PROMOTING GLOBAL INTERNET FREEDOM

INTERNET POLICIES AND ISSUES

Additional books in this series can be found on Nova's website under the Series tab.

Additional E-books in this series can be found on Nova's website under the E-books tab.

INTERNET POLICIES AND ISSUES

PROMOTING GLOBAL INTERNET FREEDOM

SAMANTHA R. WEBER
EDITOR

Nova Science Publishers, Inc.
New York

For permission to use material from this book please contact us:
Telephone 631-231-7269; Fax 631-231-8175
Web Site: http://www.novapublishers.com

LIBRARY OF CONGRESS CATALOGING-IN-PUBLICATION DATA

Promoting global Internet freedom / editors, Samantha R. Weber.
p. cm.
Includes index.
ISBN 978-1-61728-827-2 (hardcover)
1. Internet--Law and legislation--United States. 2. Human rights--United States. 3. Conditionality (International relations) 4. Human rights. I. Weber, Samantha R.
KF390.5.C6A2 2010
343.7309'944--dc22

2010025797

Published by Nova Science Publishers, Inc. ✝ New York

CONTENTS

PREFACE

Modern means of communications, led by the Internet, provide a relatively inexpensive, open, easy-entry means of sharing ideas, information, pictures, and text around the world. In a political and human rights context, in closed societies when the more established, formal news media is denied access to or does not report on specified news events, the Internet has become an alternative source of media, and sometimes a means to organize politically. The openness and the freedom of expression allowed through blogs, social networks, video sharing sites, and other tools of today's communications technology has proven to be an unprecedented and often disruptive force in some closed societies. This book provides information regarding the role of U.S. and other foreign companies in facilitating Internet censorship by repressive regimes overseas.

Chapter 1 - Modern means of communications, led by the Internet, provide a relatively inexpensive, open, easy-entry means of sharing ideas, information, pictures, and text around the world. In a political and human rights context, in closed societies when the more established, formal news media is denied access to or does not report on specified news events, the Internet has become an alternative source of media, and sometimes a means to organize politically.

The openness and the freedom of expression allowed through blogs, social networks, video sharing sites, and other tools of today's communications technology has proven to be an unprecedented and often disruptive force in some closed societies. Governments that seek to maintain their authority and control the ideas and information their citizens receive are often caught in a dilemma: they feel that they need access to the Internet to participate in commerce in the global market and for economic growth and technological development, but fear that allowing open access to the Internet potentially weakens their control over their citizens.

Legislation now under consideration in the 111th Congress would mandate that U.S. companies selling Internet technologies and services to repressive countries take actions to combat censorship and protect personally identifiable information. Some believe, however, that technology can offer a complementary and, in some cases, better and more easily implemented solution to some of those issues. They argue that hardware and Internet services, in and of themselves, are neutral elements of the Internet; it is how they are implemented by various countries that is repressive. Also, Internet services are often tailored for deployment to specific countries; however, such tailoring is done to bring the company in line with the laws of that country, not with the intention of allowing the country to repress and censor its citizenry. In many cases, that tailoring would not raise many questions about free speech and political repression.

Chapters 2 through 14 feature testimony before the U. S. House of Representatives.

In: Promoting Global Internet Freedom
Editor: Samantha R. Weber
ISBN: 978-1-61728-827-2

Chapter 1

U.S. INITIATIVES TO PROMOTE GLOBAL INTERNET FREEDOM: ISSUES, POLICY, AND TECHNOLOGY*

Patricia Moloney Figliola[1], Kennon H. Nakamura[2], Casey L. Addis[3] and Thomas Lum[4]
[1]Internet and Telecommunications Policy
[2]Foreign Affairs
[3]Middle Eastern Affairs
[4]Asian Affairs

SUMMARY

Modern means of communications, led by the Internet, provide a relatively inexpensive, open, easy-entry means of sharing ideas, information, pictures, and text around the world. In a political and human rights context, in closed societies when the more established, formal news media is denied access to or does not report on specified news events, the Internet has become an alternative source of media, and sometimes a means to organize politically.

---

* This is an edited, reformatted and augmented version of a CRS Report for Congress publication dated April 2010.

The openness and the freedom of expression allowed through blogs, social networks, video sharing sites, and other tools of today's communications technology has proven to be an unprecedented and often disruptive force in some closed societies. Governments that seek to maintain their authority and control the ideas and information their citizens receive are often caught in a dilemma: they feel that they need access to the Internet to participate in commerce in the global market and for economic growth and technological development, but fear that allowing open access to the Internet potentially weakens their control over their citizens.

Legislation now under consideration in the 111th Congress would mandate that U.S. companies selling Internet technologies and services to repressive countries take actions to combat censorship and protect personally identifiable information. Some believe, however, that technology can offer a complementary and, in some cases, better and more easily implemented solution to some of those issues. They argue that hardware and Internet services, in and of themselves, are neutral elements of the Internet; it is how they are implemented by various countries that is repressive. Also, Internet services are often tailored for deployment to specific countries; however, such tailoring is done to bring the company in line with the laws of that country, not with the intention of allowing the country to repress and censor its citizenry. In many cases, that tailoring would not raise many questions about free speech and political repression.

This report provides information regarding the role of U.S. and other foreign companies in facilitating Internet censorship by repressive regimes overseas. The report is divided into several sections:

- Examination of repressive policies in China and Iran,
- Relevant U.S. laws,
- U.S. policies to promote Internet freedom,
- Private sector initiatives, and
- Congressional action.

Two appendixes describe technologies and mechanisms for censorship and circumvention of government restrictions.

INTRODUCTION

In the late 1960s and 1970s, advancements in telecommunications technologies enabled the creation of a large-scale, interconnected network called ARPANET ("Advanced Research Projects Agency Network"). ARPANET was created by the Defense Advanced Research Projects Agency as a government-funded enterprise until the mid-1990s, when it began commercialization. Today's Internet is a direct outgrowth of the technologies developed and lessons learned from ARPANET. During the late 1990s, the Internet began having a significant impact on culture and commerce, including the exponential increase of near instant communication by electronic mail (e-mail), text-based discussion forums, and the graphical World Wide Web.

Today, the Internet has evolved even further and many people are using newer tools, such as blogs, social networks, video sharing sites, and other aspects of today's communications technology to express their political ideals, many times in conflict with the political opinions and outlook espoused by their governments. In this way, the Internet has proven to be an unprecedented and often disruptive force in some closed societies, as the governments seek to maintain their authority and control the ideas and information their citizens receive. These regimes are often caught in a dilemma: they need the Internet to participate in commerce in the global market and for economic growth and technological development, but they also seek to restrict the Internet in order to maintain the government's control. Figure 3 illustrates an assessment by Freedom House[1] of the extent to which selected countries restrict freedom on the Internet.

In Burma during the 2007 Saffron Revolution, YouTube footage, often filmed with cell phone cameras, conveyed to the world the human rights violations against the monks and generated international awareness and reaction. Demonstrations in Tehran following the June 12, 2009, presidential elections were often organized through Twitter and text messages over cell phones.

The Iranian government's violent response to the demonstrations was spread around the world through live cell phone pictures, e-mails, and phone calls. The Voice of America (VOA) reported that during the demonstrations, Iranians sent VOA over 300 videos a day, along with thousands of still pictures, e-mails, and telephone calls to the agency.[2]

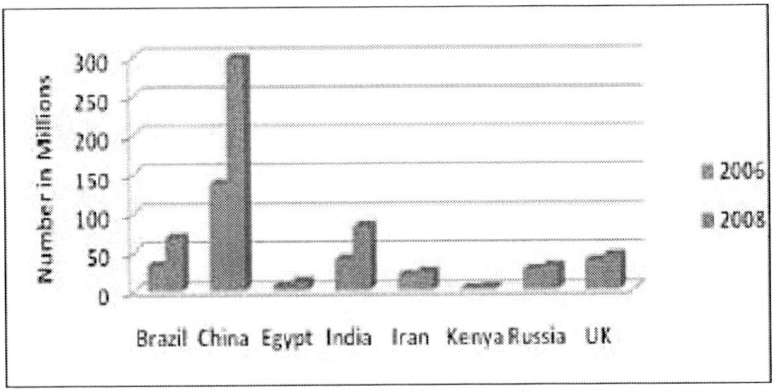

Source: "Freedom on the Net: A Global Assessment of Internet and Digital Media," Freedom House, April 1, 2009.

Figure 1. Growth in Number of Internet Users in Select Countries 2006-2008

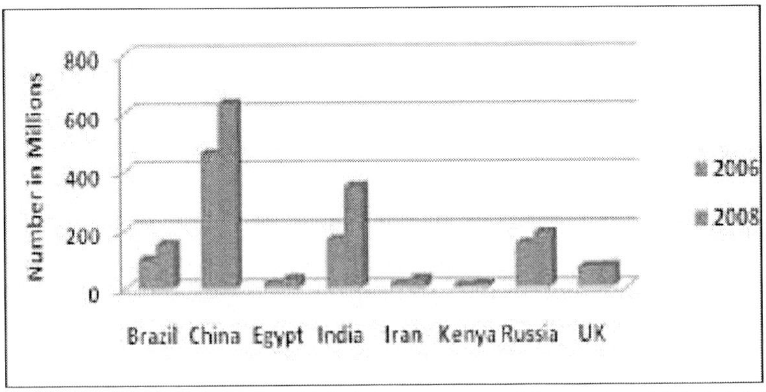

Source: "Freedom on the Net: A Global Assessment of Internet and Digital Media," Freedom House, April 1, 2009.

Figure 2. Growth in Mobile Phone Access in Select Countries 2006-2008

A variety of control mechanisms are employed by regimes seeking to limit the ways the Internet is used, ranging from sophisticated surveillance and censorship to threats of retaliation (which foster self-censorship) and actual harassment and arrests of Internet users. Such regimes often require the assistance of foreign Internet companies operating in their countries. These global technology companies find themselves in a dilemma. They often must choose between following the laws and the requests of authorities of the host country, or refusing to do so and risking the loss of business licenses or the ability to sell services in that country.

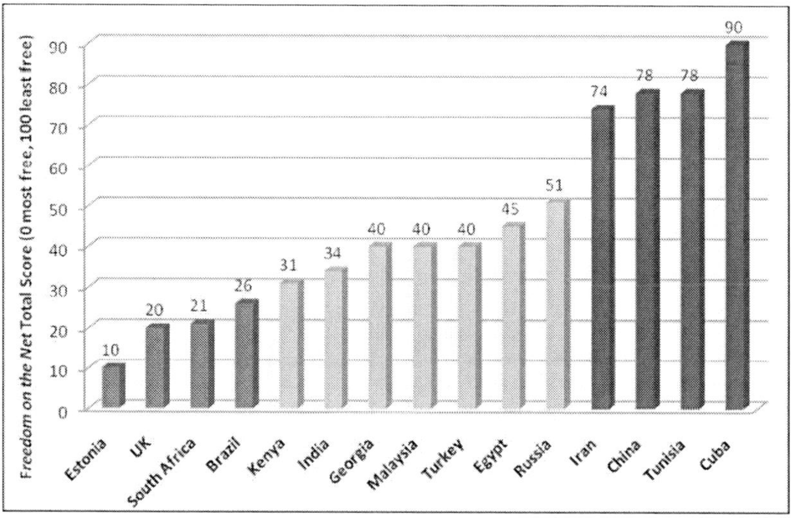

Source: "Freedom on the Net: A Global Assessment of Internet and Digital Media," Freedom House, April 1, 2009

Notes: Estonia to Brazil are "Free." Kenya to Russia are "Partly Free." Iran to Cuba are "Not Free."

Figure 3. Freedom on the Net 15 Country Comparison (0 Best, 100 Worst)

Human rights groups have protested that Yahoo! and Google censor and remove material deemed sensitive by host governments on country-specific search engines.[3] Microsoft is said to censor Chinese versions of its blog platforms.[4] Human rights groups also charge that Yahoo! has provided Chinese authorities personal identifying information about users that has allowed the government to identify and arrest individuals for statements made on the Web.[5] A representative of Google, Inc. acknowledged the problem of government involvement, noting.

> As our ... Burma experiences indicate, our products are platforms for free expression, transparency, and accountability. Because of this, we often face efforts by governments throughout the world to restrict or deny access to our products.[6]

The Global Online Freedom Act of 2009 (GOFA) (H.R. 2271), introduced by Representative Christopher Smith, would mandate that companies selling Internet technologies and services to repressive countries take actions to combat censorship and protect personally identifiable information. Some believe, however, that technology can offer a complementary and, in some cases, better and more easily implemented solution to prevent government censorship. Hardware and Internet services, in and of themselves, are neutral elements of the Internet; it is how they are implemented by various countries that makes Internet access "repressive."

For example, hardware, such as routers, is needed to provide Internet service everywhere. However, hardware features intended for day-to-day Internet traffic management, conducted by Internet service providers (ISPs) and governments for benign purposes, can be misused. Repressive governments are able to use these features to censor traffic and monitor use—sometimes using them to identify specific individuals for prosecution. It is not currently feasible to remove those features from the product, even when sold to countries that use those features to repress political speech.[7]

On the other hand, Internet services, such as Google, are often tailored for deployment to specific countries. Such tailoring is done to bring the company's products and services in line with the laws of that country, and not with the end goal of allowing the country to repress and censor its citizenry. In many cases, tailoring does not raise many questions about free speech and political repression because the country is not considered to be a repressive regime. Under Canadian human rights law, for example, it is illegal to promote violence against protected groups; therefore, when reported, Google.ca will remove such links from search results.[8]

Internet censorship and the prosecution of individuals who attempt to circumvent that censorship are unlikely to be eliminated in some countries. However, while some governments are continually looking for new and more thorough methods to restrict or inhibit Internet use, citizens in these countries are active in developing techniques to circumvent those efforts.

Examples of Countries Charged with Restricting Internet Freedom

The organization Reporters Without Borders has listed 15 countries where Internet freedom is restricted. These countries are China, Cuba, North Korea, Belarus, Myanmar, Egypt, Ethiopia, Iran, Saudi Arabia, Syria, Tunisia, Turkmenistan, Uzbekistan, Vietnam, and Zimbabwe.[9] This report covers two of these countries, China and Iran, both of which have been in the news during 2009 and 2010.

China[10]

The People's Republic of China (PRC) has the world's largest number of Internet users, estimated at 330 million people, including 70 million bloggers. It also has one of the most sophisticated and aggressive Internet censorship and control regimes in the world. According to some estimates, between 30 and 40 Chinese citizens are serving prison sentences for writing about politically sensitive topics online.[11] In November 2009, Huang Qi, a human rights advocate, was sentenced to three years in prison for "possessing state secrets" after posting online appeals and complaints of families whose children had been killed in school buildings during the Sichuan earthquake of May 2008. Some studies show that the vast majority of Internet users in China do not view the medium as a political tool.[12] Nonetheless, Chinese Internet users are able to access unprecedented amounts of information, despite government attempts to limit the flow, while political activists and others continue to push back against restrictions and find ways to circumvent censorship.

PRC officials have argued that Internet controls are necessary for social stability and that new restrictions target pornography and other "harmful content."[13] Chinese official commentary has suggested that the U.S. government has applied a double standard, regulating the Internet at home while calling for other countries to eliminate controls. The PRC government also has referred to U.S. criticism of Internet restrictions in China as politically motivated and an interference in China's domestic affairs.[14]

The PRC government employs a variety of methods to control online content and expression, including website blocking and keyword filtering; regulating and monitoring Internet service providers, Internet cafes, and university bulletin board systems; registering websites and blogs; and occasional arrests of high-profile "cyber dissidents" or crackdowns on Internet service providers.[15] Some analysts argue that even though the PRC government cannot control all Internet content and use, its selective targeting creates an undercurrent of fear and promotes self- censorship. Blocked websites, social networking sites, and file sharing sites include Radio Free Asia, international human rights websites, many Taiwanese newspapers, Facebook, Twitter, and YouTube. The government reportedly has hired thousands of students to express pro-government views on websites, bulletin boards, and chat rooms.[16] Furthermore, some analysts argue that the Internet has enhanced government propaganda and surveillance capabilities.

Nonetheless, the Internet has made it impossible for the Chinese government to restrict information as fully as before; bulletin boards, comment boards, chat rooms, blogs, and other outlets have allowed for an unprecedented amount of information and public comment on social and other issues. Although the state has the capability to block news of events or to partially shut down the Internet, as it did in Xinjiang following ethnic unrest that erupted there in July 2009, it often cannot do so before such events are publicized, if only fleetingly, online. The threat of public exposure or condemnation through the Internet reportedly has compelled some government officials to conduct affairs more openly. For Chinese Internet users in search of censored information, circumventing government controls is often made possible by way of "proxy servers" or "virtual private networks" using special software.[17] Furthermore, English language news sites, such as the *New York Times* and the *Washington Post*, are generally available.

U.S. Internet Companies, China, and Human Rights Issues

Some human rights activists and U.S. policy makers have expressed concern that U.S. Internet companies have sold Internet services or technologies to China that have assisted the PRC government in restricting information and communication and in monitoring and identifying Internet users. U.S. congressional committees and commissions have held hearings on the topics of global Internet freedom and the roles of U.S. Internet and technology companies in China's censorship regime. Some media watchdog groups and Members of Congress have maintained that some U.S. information technology companies, including Yahoo!, Microsoft, Google, and Cisco Systems, have provided willing, direct, sustained, or comprehensive support to PRC Internet censorship and political control efforts.[18]

U.S. information technology companies have responded that they must abide by the laws of the countries in which they operate, and that they are not actively cooperating or collaborating with the PRC government or tailoring their products to suit PRC censorship requirements.[19] These companies add that despite PRC censorship policies, they nonetheless are enlarging the volume of information available in China and other Internet-restricting countries, and can better press for freedom of expression and protection of privacy while located in these countries. They also claim that Chinese and other Asian and European competitors would fill the void in providing Internet services and technology in their absence. Furthermore, some Chinese experts have suggested that overall, the Internet, including foreign involvement, has created greater political freedom, despite the ongoing battle against growing PRC government attempts to control it.[20]

Yahoo!

Yahoo! has been blamed for complicity in the arrests of at least four Chinese Internet users by providing their e-mail account information to PRC authorities. In the most high-profile case, in 2004, Yahoo!'s Hong Kong office was accused of having provided information about the identity of a Chinese journalist and Yahoo! e-mail account holder, Shi Tao. Shi reportedly had forwarded information about state policy regarding the 15th anniversary of the Tiananmen demonstrations via his Yahoo! e-mail account to an overseas democracy group.[21] In March 2005, a PRC court sentenced Shi to 10 years in prison for "leaking state secrets." In August 2005, Yahoo! bought a 39% stake in China's Alibaba Group, a Chinese Internet service provider, and turned over its PRC operations to the Chinese company.

Microsoft

In 2005, Microsoft shut down the MSN Spaces site of Chinese political blogger Zhao Jing (a.k.a. Michael Anti) at the request of the PRC government, after Zhao had expressed support in his blog for a boycott of *Beijing News* following the firing of one of its editors. Human rights activists also criticized Microsoft for blocking words such as "democracy" from MSN Spaces. Microsoft was China's leading blog service provider at the time and remains one of the most popular. Recently, Microsoft also has been accused of cooperating with China's censorship policies in the development of its new *Bing* search engine.[22]

Google

Google's activities in China have reflected an attempt by the company to comply with PRC policies while limiting the company's role in censorship. Google's Chinese search engine, Google.cn, reportedly is the second-most widely used information-gathering service in China after that of *Baidu*, a Chinese company, and is the least censored, according to one study.[23] Google.cn provides a message stating that a website is unavailable due to "local laws, regulations, and policies," suggesting to the user that additional information exists, but that the government has closed access to that site. In 2006, Google reportedly moved its search records outside of the PRC in order to prevent the government from accessing the data without the company's consent, and does not host Gmail and Blogger services in China as a measure to protect the privacy of Chinese account holders.[24]

Ever since it entered the China market in 2005, Google and the PRC government have clashed over censorship and other issues, although the company has complied with Chinese laws in principle. In June 2009, China's Foreign Ministry accused the Internet company of violating PRC law and enabling Chinese Internet users to access "vulgar content." Google's Chinese service was disrupted for a few days, which some analysts viewed as the Chinese government response to Google's apparent resistance to abide by new censorship edicts.[25] Chinese writers accused Google of copyright infringement after the company began publishing their works in its online library, Google Books.[26] In October 2009, the *People's Daily,* the state's premier newspaper, accused Google of blocking its stories of the dispute.

Cisco Systems

Cicso Systems, Juniper Networks, Nortel of Canada, and Alcatel of France reportedly were involved in upgrading China's Internet infrastructure, filtering, and surveillance systems earlier this decade. According to some reports, Cisco Systems sold several thousand routers to China, which helped to facilitate the PRC government's censorship of Internet content and monitoring of Internet users.[27] According to other reports, Cisco sold technology to China's police force that can be used in the collection and use of data regarding personal background and imaging information, Web browsing history, and e-mail.[28]

The Continuing Battle between Censorship and Freedom of Information

The PRC government has displayed a growing nervousness about the Internet's influence on Chinese society and politics, but it has been reluctant to provoke the ire of China's online population or to reduce the attractiveness of China's business environment for foreign investors. In June 2009, the PRC government issued a directive requiring "Green Dam Youth Escort" software, designed to prevent children from accessing "harmful content," such as pornography, on all Chinese computers sold after July 1, 2009, including those imported from abroad. Many Chinese Internet users, international human rights activists, foreign governments, chambers of commerce, and information technology manufacturers openly opposed the policy, arguing that the software would undermine computer operability, that it could be used to expand censorship to include political content, and that it could incorporate pirated software and weaken Internet security.[29] On June 30, 2009, the PRC government announced that mandatory installation of the software would be delayed for an indefinite period. On August 14, 2009, Minister of Industry and Information Technology Li Yizhong stated that the directive had created misunderstandings and that, "We will listen to the public's views before issuing a new directive on Green Dam."[30]

Following the aborted launch of "Green Dam," the PRC government has continued to tighten controls over Internet content and use, but in a quieter manner. In September 2009, PRC authorities issued requirements that new users register their true identities. This regulation reportedly has not been well enforced; however, the government can still track down individuals through their IP addresses. In December 2009, new restrictions aimed at cracking down on pornography, media piracy, and threats to national security and stability resulted in the closing of hundreds of websites, many of them entertainment-oriented. Furthermore, the China Internet Network Information Center announced that individuals could no longer apply for ".cn" domain names (China's country code), which it would now limit to registered business enterprises. Some observers argued that these policies could dampen the richness and vibrancy of Internet content and activity in China, as well as provoke a public backlash.[31] On October 15, 2009 (Internet Human Rights Day), 15 Chinese intellectuals issued a Declaration of Internet Human Rights calling for freedom of opinion, speech, and publication online.[32]

Google and Cyber Attacks

In January 2010, Google threatened to cease censoring its Chinese search engine or to pull out of China. The company asserted that, in December 2009, Chinese hackers had attacked its Gmail service and corporate network as well as the computer systems of many other large U.S. corporations in the PRC.[33] Hackers appeared to have targeted the Gmail accounts of Chinese human rights activists; the intellectual property, including "source codes" or programming languages, of Google and other companies; and information on U.S. weapons systems. In a statement, Google's chief legal officer announced that the company would no longer censor results on Google.cn, even if that meant having to shut down the search engine, and potentially its offices in China.[34] Yahoo!, which was also hit by Chinese hackers, expressed support for Google's actions, thereby provoking an angry response by its PRC partner, *Alibaba*.

Chinese discussion boards and micro-blog postings indicated that a small majority of China's online population—and perhaps a large majority of its most active Internet users—wanted Google to stay in China, with some supporting Google's challenge to the PRC government. A significant minority adopted a pro-government stance or interpreted Google's move as profit-oriented.[35] According to some analysts, although China has huge potential, the company currently earns an estimated $300 million to $400 million from its China operations, a "tiny fraction" of its $22 billion in sales worldwide.[36]

While visiting Shanghai during his state visit to China in November 2009, President Barack Obama expressed support of unrestricted Internet access and disapproval of censorship. On January 21, 2010, in a policy speech on Internet freedom, Secretary of State Hillary Clinton urged U.S. Internet companies to oppose censorship in their overseas operations and announced that the Global Internet Freedom Taskforce (GIFT) would be reinvigorated. She also called upon the PRC government to conduct a thorough investigation of the December 2009 cyberattacks upon U.S. companies in China and to make its results transparent. Beijing denied involvement in the attacks and defended its Internet policies. The Foreign Ministry stated that foreign companies, including Google, "should respect the laws and regulations, respect the public interest of Chinese people and China's culture and customs and shoulder due social responsibilities."[37]

Iran[38]

The Iranian government has restricted Internet usage since access spread beyond universities and government agencies to the general population in the late 1990s. Today, Iran has an estimated 23 million Internet users,[39] and watchdog groups and Internet activists claim that Iran's filtering and monitoring of usage is among the most extensive in the world. Additional information about Iran's Internet policies is available from the U.S. Department of State in its annual report, *2008 Country Reports on Human Rights Practices*.

The Iranian government tracks online communication and content through a centralized location in the state's telecommunications monopoly, the Ministry of Communications and Information Technology (MCIT). In addition to its 23 million Internet users, the Persian blogosphere is among the world's most robust. The status of Internet sites and blogs remains contested under Iranian law, but the Press Law does require that bloggers obtain licenses, and all content on websites and blogs is subject to approval of the Ministry of Culture and Islamic Guidance (MCIG). The government also regulates access to the Internet by limiting the speed of Internet access that ISPs can provide to households and public access sites (Internet cafes) to 128 kilobytes per second, making it difficult or impossible to download multimedia content. Iran reportedly is the only country to have imposed a cap on Internet access speed for households.[40] Iran also has arrested numerous activists, bloggers, and journalists on charges of "antigovernment publicity," "propaganda against the Islamic Republic," and "jeopardizing national security."[41]

The government has disabled the Internet altogether in the past, usually during elections, but some observers argue that improvements in monitoring and filtering technologies have made such measures unnecessary and even enabled the government to use the Internet to disseminate disinformation and pro-government content. Following the disputed 2009 presidential election, the Internet was reportedly slow but accessible. The number of detentions of Internet activists and bloggers increased during the post-election unrest, arguably demonstrating the extent of government filtering and monitoring of usage. The post-election crackdown on Internet freedom raised concerns that Iran's human rights abuses were being aided by Western technology companies. Others said the concerns were being overstated, asserting that Iran also develops its own filtering and monitoring technologies.

The Nokia Siemens Network (NSN)[42] sold communication monitoring equipment to the Iranian government in 2008.[43] The monitoring center, installed into the MCIT gateway, was part of a larger contract with Iran that included mobile phone network technology. The Iranian government had reportedly experimented with the monitoring equipment prior to the election, but did not use it extensively until after the election. Some experts have argued that the nature of the content inspection happening in Iran since the election goes beyond the practices of other countries, including China.[44]

NSN maintains that it sold the technology for the purpose of "lawful intercept" of information used to track criminals and terrorists.[45] Critics argue that in a country like Iran, where the population is heavily reliant on Internet communication with the outside world due to censorship of other communication, this technology enables the government to intensify repression.[46]

U.S. Law and Internet Freedom Abroad[47]

In response to laws and regulations of foreign countries requiring censorship and disclosure of users' personal information, some U.S.

technology firms engage in Internet censoring and filtering. Some examples include China and other Internet-restricting countries such as Iran. In some cases, such as in Iran, Internet censoring and filtering reportedly involve a practice often called deep packet inspection which is under a great deal of scrutiny in the United States.[48] Doing business in a foreign country subjects the business to the jurisdiction of that country.[49] Nonetheless, concerns have been raised that China's Internet filtering could run afoul of world trade obligations.[50]

U.S. Policy for the Promotion of Internet Freedom Abroad[51]

The importance of Internet freedom to the United States was declared in 2006. During an explanation of that year's State Department 2006 *Country Reports on Human Rights Practices*, then-Under Secretary of State for Democracy and Global Affairs Paula J. Dobriansky explained that the 2006 reports included new, additional focus on "the extent to which internet access is available to and used by citizens in each country and ... whether governments inappropriately limit or block access to the internet or censor websites."[52] This was added as an area of concern because the internet is playing a growing role in people's ability to freely express themselves and in the free flow of information. In discussing this new area of focus, then-Under Secretary Dobriansky said,

> We will continue to defend internet freedom, including by addressing internet repression directly with the foreign governments involved and seeking to persuade foreign officials that restricting internet freedom is contrary to their own interests and that of their countries. The new information in this year's reports will make an important contribution.[53]

At this same time, then-Secretary of State Condoleezza Rice also established the Global Internet Freedom Task Force (GIFT) in order to provide a U.S. foreign policy response to violations of Internet freedom by repressive regimes around the world.[54]

Secretary of State Hillary Rodham Clinton, in a January 21, 2010, speech, stated that Internet freedom is a central part of U.S. foreign policy. She stated that Internet freedom is more than a question of information freedom, it is about the nature of the world we want to inhabit. Clinton further stated: "It's about whether we live on a planet with one Internet, one global community, and a common body of knowledge that benefits and unites us all, or a fragmented planet in which access to information and opportunity is dependent on where you live and the whims of censors."[55]

In her remarks, Secretary Clinton placed the United States on the side of a single Internet where everyone has equal access to knowledge and ideas. She noted that blogs, e-mails, social networks, and text messages are opening up a new virtual town square where citizens can go to criticize their governments and exchange ideas. U.S. responsibility to support this new "town square" is not new but can be found in the First Amendment of the U.S. Bill of Rights ensuring freedom of speech, assembly, and religion. Secretary Clinton argued that these principles were reaffirmed in President Franklin Roosevelt's "The Four Freedoms" speech,[56] and in the work of the United States and its support of the Universal Declaration of Human Rights.

Secretary Clinton further explained that U.S. foreign policy is premised on the idea that no country stands to benefit more than the United States when there is cooperation among peoples and states. No country shoulders a heavier burden than the United States when conflict and misunderstanding make the international system unstable, and force people and countries apart. She stated that it is important that the United States seizes the opportunities that come with interconnectivity and work for a world in which access to networks and information brings people closer together and expands the definition of the global community.

Secretary Clinton continued the GIFT and its responsibilities. The Task Force is co-chaired by the Under Secretaries of State for Democracy and Global Affairs and for Economic, Business, and Agricultural Affairs and draws on the State Department's multidisciplinary expertise in its regional and functional bureaus to work on issues such as international communications, human rights, democratization, business advocacy and corporate social responsibility, and country specific concerns. The task force supports Internet freedom by[57]

- monitoring Internet freedom and reporting in its annual *Country Reports on Human Rights Practices* the quality of Internet freedom in each country around the world;
- responding in both bilateral and international fora to support Internet freedom; and
- expanding access to the Internet with greater technical and financial support for increasing availability of the Internet in the developing world.

In advancing Internet freedom as an objective of U.S. foreign policy, Secretary Clinton proposed a number of key initiatives:[58]

- Continue the work of the State Department's GIFT as it oversees U.S. efforts in more than 40 countries to help individuals circumvent politically motivated censorship by developing new tools and providing the training needed to safely access the Internet;
- Make Internet freedom an issue at the United Nations and the U.N. Human Rights Council in order to enlist world opinion and support for Internet Freedom;
- Work with new partners in industry, academia, and non-governmental organizations to establish a standing effort to advance the power of "connection technologies" that will empower citizens and leverage U.S. traditional diplomacy;
- Provide new, competitive grants for ideas and applications that help break down communications barriers, overcome illiteracy, and connect people to servers and information they need;
- Urge and work with U.S. media companies to take a proactive role in challenging foreign governments' demands for censorship and surveillance; and
- Encourage the voluntary work of the communications-oriented, private sector-led Global Network Initiative (GNI). The GNI brings technology companies, nongovernmental organizations, academic experts, and social investment funds together to develop responses and mechanisms to government requests for censorship.

To fund U.S. efforts in support of Internet freedom, Congress in FY2008 appropriated $15 million, most of which has been spent or is obligated. Another $5 million was appropriated in FY2009. Finally, in Secretary Clinton's January 21 speech, she spoke of an additional $15 million for FY20 10 that has been allocated from State Department appropriations to a range of programs that, in full or in part, support Internet freedom. Assistant Secretary for Democracy, Human Rights, and Labor Michael Posner describes these programs as "not just circumvention.... [I]t's a lot about training people.... It's some about technology. It's some about encouraging groups that are in danger. It's a lot about diplomacy, too, for us getting out there and being sure that when groups are in trouble, we provide a lifeline."[59]

The U.S. Broadcasting Board of Governors' International Broadcasting Bureau also supports counter-censorship technologies and has committed approximately $2 million per year to help enable Internet users in repressive regimes to have access to the VOA and other U.S. governmental and non-governmental websites and to receive VOA e-mail newsletters.

Some observers have expressed concerns that there could be serious negative consequences for U.S. and foreign companies, and U.S. or foreign nationals working or living in countries with repressive regimes, if they follow the expanded U.S. policy supporting Internet freedom. These commenters point out that repressive governments could punish or make an example of an individual or company for not following the dictates of that country. Such actions could include harassment, lifting of business licenses, confiscation of assets, or imprisonment. These observers question what powers, beyond expressing U.S. displeasure through official demarches and public statements or through negotiations, that the United States may have to respond to such actions.[60]

Congressional Action

In 2010, Congress has taken steps to address ongoing concerns about ensuring the free and secure flow of information over the Internet:

- On March 10, 2010, the House Committee on Foreign Affairs conducted a hearing, "The Google Predicament: Transforming U.S. Cyberspace Policy to Advance Democracy, Security, and Trade," on the December 2009 Chinese cyber attacks on Google and other U.S. companies, to consider policy tools to address Internet freedom, trade, and cyber security issues;
- On March 9, 2010, Representatives David Wu and Christopher Smith announced the formation of the House Global Internet Freedom Caucus; and
- The Senate Judiciary Committee, Subcommittee on Human Rights and the Law, held a hearing on March 2, 2010, entitled "Global Internet Freedom and the Rule of Law, Part II" to examine human rights, corporate responsibility, and other issues related to Internet censorship around the world.

The Global Network Initiative: Private Sector Support of Internet Freedom[61]

The Global Network Initiative (GNI) was formed in October 2008 to respond to criticism of Internet service providers and computer manufacturers who had sold technology or services to Internet-restricting countries.[62] GNI was launched by a coalition of human rights organizations, academics, investors and technology leaders. GNI adopts a self-regulatory approach to protect and advance individuals' rights to free expression and privacy on the Internet. A set of principles and supporting mechanisms provide guidance to the information and communications technology (ICT) industry and its stakeholders on how to protect and advance the human rights of freedom of expression and privacy when faced with pressures from governments to take actions that infringe upon these rights.

Governments are not members of the GNI, but are encouraged to support the principles and encourage their adoption. Organizations participating in the GNI include Google Inc., Microsoft Corp., and Yahoo! Inc. Each initial participating company committed $100,000 per year over the two-year start-up period. Organizations not participating in the initiative who where involved in its development include Amnesty International and Reporters Without Borders. Reporters Without Borders remains skeptical about how much change GNI can effect, and pushed for standards that would require all government requests and takedown notices be made in writing.

The GNI's Principles on Freedom of Expression and Privacy ("the Principles") are based on internationally recognized laws and standards for human rights, including the Universal Declaration of Human Rights (UDHR), the International Covenant on Civil and Political Rights (ICCPR) and the International Covenant on Economic, Social, and Cultural Rights.

The GNI acknowledges that the rights of privacy and of freedom of expression should not be restricted by governments, except in narrowly defined circumstances based on internationally recognized laws or standards. The Implementation Guidelines ("The Guidelines") of the GNI provide guidance to ICT companies on how to implement the Principles, and describe the actions that constitute compliance.

With respect to government demands to remove or limit access to content or restrict communications, participating companies commit to encourage governments to

- be specific, transparent, and consistent in the demands issued to restrict freedom of expression online;
- encourage government demands that are consistent with international laws and standards;
- require governments to follow local legal processes, interpret government demands so as to minimize the negative effect, when required to restrict communications or remove content; and
- interpret the governmental authority's jurisdiction to minimize the negative effect.

Participating companies commit to operate in a transparent manner when required to remove content or restrict access, and must disclose to users the applicable laws and policies requiring such action, the company's policies for responding to government demands, and provide timely notice to users when access to content has been locked or communications limited due to government restrictions. With respect to privacy, participating companies commit to assess the human rights risks associated with the collection, storage, and retention of personal information and to develop mitigation strategies.

A system of independent third-party assessment of company compliance with the Principles and Implementation Guidelines will be phased in over three stages:

- In Phase One (ends December 2010) each participating company establishes internal policies and procedures to implement the Principles, and the Board approves independence and competence criteria for the selection of independent assessors.
- In Phase Two (2011) independent assessors will conduct process assessments of each participating company to review and evaluate their internal systems for implementing the Principles.
- In Phase Three (January 2012 onwards) the Board will accredit independent assessors to review the internal systems of companies, and company responses to specific government demands implicating freedom of expression or privacy. Each participating company will submit an annual report to the Organization. The assessors will prepare reports explaining each company's responses to government demands, evaluating the effectiveness of the company's responses. Each company will be given the opportunity to respond to the assessor's draft and final report. The Board of the Organization will assess whether the company is in compliance with the Principles and

its determination will be made public. The Board of the Organization will publish an annual report assessing each participating company's compliance with the Principles.

RECENT LEGISLATIVE ACTION[63]

Public Laws

H.R. 2647, *National Defense Authorization Act for Fiscal Year 2010*. Introduced by Representative Skelton (by request), referred to the House Armed Services Committee. Enacted October 28, 2009, P.L. 111-84.

Title XII: Matters Relating to Foreign Nations

Subtitle D: VOICE Act - Victims of Iranian Censorship Act or VOICE Act

(Sec. 1242) Expresses the sense of the Senate in support of the universal values of freedom of speech, the press, and expression as it pertains to the people of Iran, and condemns acts of censorship, intimidation, and other restrictions on such freedom in Iran.

(Sec. 1243) States that it shall be the policy of the United States to (1) support freedom of the press, speech, expression, and assembly in Iran; (2) support the Iranian people as they seek, receive, and impart information and promote ideas in writing, print, and through other media; (3) discourage businesses from aiding efforts to interfere with the ability of the Iranian people to access or share information or otherwise infringe upon such freedoms; and (4) encourage the development of technologies that facilitate efforts of the Iranian people to share such information, exercise such freedoms, and engage in Internet-based education programs and other exchanges between U.S. citizens and Iranians.

(Sec. 1244) Authorizes appropriations for the (1) International Broadcasting Operations Fund to expand Farsi language programming and to disseminate accurate and independent information to the Iranian people through radio, television, Internet, cellular telephone, short message service, and other communications; and (2) Broadcasting Capital Improvements Fund to expand transmissions of Farsi language programs to Iran.

(Sec. 1245) Establishes in the Treasury the Iranian Electronic Education, Exchange, and Media Fund to support the development of technologies that will aid the Iranian people in exchanging information and exercising freedom of speech, expression, and assembly. Authorizes appropriations to the Fund.

(Sec. 1246) Directs the President to report annually to Congress on the use of funds authorized under this Subtitle.

(Sec. 1247) Requires the President to (1) direct the appropriate officials to examine claims that non-Iranian companies have provided hardware, software, or other forms of assistance to the government of Iran that has furthered its efforts to filter online political content, disrupt cell phone and Internet communications, and monitor the online activities of Iranian citizens; and (2) report study results to Congress.

(Sec. 1248) Authorizes appropriations to the Secretary of State to document, collect, and disseminate information about human rights in Iran, including abuses since the Iranian presidential election on June 12, 2009.

Bills and Resolutions in the House of Representatives

H.R. 2271, *Global Online Freedom Act of 2009*. Introduced by Representative Christopher Smith and referred to the House Committee on Foreign Affairs; and the House Committee on Energy and Commerce.

Makes it U.S. policy to (1) promote the freedom to seek, receive, and impart information and ideas through any media; (2) use all appropriate instruments of U.S. influence to support the free flow of information without interference or discrimination; and (3) deter U.S. businesses from cooperating with Internet-restricting countries in effecting online censorship.

Expresses the sense of Congress that (1) the President should seek international agreements to protect Internet freedom; and (2) some U.S. businesses, in assisting foreign governments to restrict online access to U.S.-supported websites and government reports and to identify individual Internet users, are working contrary to U.S. foreign policy interests.

Amends the Foreign Assistance Act of 1961 to require assessments of electronic information freedom in each foreign country.

Establishes in the Department of State the Office of Global Internet Freedom (OGIF).

Directs the Secretary of State to annually designate Internet-restricting countries. Prohibits, subject to waiver, U.S. businesses that provide to the public a commercial Internet search engine, communications services, or hosting services from locating, in such countries, any personally identifiable information used to establish or maintain an Internet services account.

Requires U.S. businesses that collect or obtain personally identifiable information through the Internet to notify the OGIF and the Attorney General before responding to a disclosure request from an Internet-restricting country. Authorizes the Attorney General to prohibit a business from complying with the request, except for legitimate foreign law enforcement purposes.

Requires U.S. businesses to report to the OGIF certain Internet censorship information involving Internet-restricting countries.

Prohibits U.S. businesses that maintain Internet content hosting services from jamming U.S.- supported web sites or U.S.-supported content in Internet-restricting countries.

Authorizes the President to waive provisions of this act: (1) to further the purposes of this act; (2) if a country ceases restrictive activity; or (3) if it is the national interest of the United States.

H.R. 4784,[64] *Internet Freedom Act of 2010*. Introduced by Representative Wu and referred to the House Science and Technology Committee, Subcommittee on Research and Science Education.

Directs the National Science Foundation to establish the Internet Freedom Foundation governed by a board of 12 members, with equal representation from government, academia, and the private sector. The Internet Freedom Foundation shall—

- Award competitive, merit-reviewed grants, cooperative agreements, or contracts to private industry, universities, and other research and development organizations to develop deployable technologies to defeat Internet suppression and censorship; and
- Award incentive prizes to private industry, universities, and other research and development organizations that successfully develop deployable technologies to defeat Internet suppression and censorship.

The Internet Freedom Foundation shall be funded by such sums as may be necessary.

H.Res. 590, *Expressing grave concerns about the sweeping censorship, privacy, and cybersecurity implications of China's Green Dam filtering software, and urging U.S. high-tech companies to promote the Internet as a* *tool for transparency, freedom of expression, and citizen empowerment around the world.* Introduced by Representative Wu and referred to the House Committee on Foreign Affairs.

Expresses (1) grave concerns about the sweeping censorship, privacy, and cybersecurity implications of China's Green Dam filtering software; and (2) support for the Chinese people in their quest for Internet freedom and free expression.

Calls on (1) the Chinese government to rescind its requirement for Green Dam to be preinstalled on all new computers; and (2) U.S. high-tech companies to promote the Internet as a tool for transparency, freedom of expression, and citizen empowerment around the world.

H.Res. 672, *Calling on the Government of the Socialist Republic of Vietnam to release imprisoned bloggers and respect Internet freedom.* Introduced by Representative Sanchez and referred to the House Committee on Foreign Affairs. Passed on October 21, 2009.

Supports the right of the citizens of the Socialist Republic of Vietnam to access websites of their choosing and to have the freedom to share and publish information over the Internet.

Calls on Vietnam to (1) repeal Circular 07, Article 88, and similar statutes that restrict the Internet, so as to be in line with the International Covenant on Civil and Political Rights, to which Vietnam is a signatory; (2) become a responsible member state of the international community by respecting individuals' freedom of speech, freedom of press, and freedom of political association; and (3) release all political prisoners, including but not limited to 18 named bloggers and cyber activists.

Appendix A. Technologies Used to Monitor and Censor Web Sites and Web-Based Communications[65]

Key-Word List Blocking

This is a simple type of filtration where a government drops any Internet packets featuring certain keywords, such as "protest" or "proxy."

Domain Name System (DNS) Poisoning

DNS poisoning intentionally introduces errors into the Internet's directory service to misdirect the original request to another IP address.

IP Blocking

IP Blocking is one of the most basic methods that governments use for censorship, as it simply prevents all packets going to or from targeted IP addresses. This is an easy technology to implement, but it does not address the problem of individual communications between users. This method is used to block banned websites, including news sites and proxy servers that would allow access to banned content, from being viewed.

Bandwidth Throttling

Bandwidth throttling simply limits the amount of traffic that can be sent over the Internet. Keeping data volume low facilitates other methods of monitoring and filtering by limiting the amount of data present.

Traffic Classification

This is a much more sophisticated method of blocking traffic than IP blocking, as governments can halt any file sent through a certain type of protocol, such as FTP. Because the government knows that FTP transfers are most often sent through TCP port 21, they can simply limit the bandwidth available on that port and throttle transfers. This type of traffic-shaping practice is the most common one used by repressive governments today. It is not resource intensive and it is fairly easy to implement.

Shallow Packet Inspection (SPI)

Shallow packet inspection is a less sophisticated version of the deep packet inspection (DPI) technique (DPI is described below) that is used to block packets based on their content. Unlike DPI, which intercepts packets and inspects their fingerprints (fingerprinting is described below), headers, and payloads, SPI makes broad generalities about traffic based solely on evaluating the packet header. Although shallow packet inspection can't provide the same refined/detailed traffic assessments as DPI, it is much better at handling volume than DPI.

SPI is much less refined than DPI, but it is capable of handling a greater volume of traffic much more quickly. SPI is akin to judging a book by its cover. This method is prone to exploitation by users because they can disguise their packets to look like a different kind of traffic.

Packet Fingerprinting

This is a slightly more refined method of throttling packets than shallow packet inspection, as it looks not only at the packet header but at its length, frequency of transmission, and other characteristics to make a rough determination of its content. In this manner, the government can better classify packets and not throttle traffic sent out by key businesses.

Deep Packet Inspection (DPI) / Packet Content Filtering

DPI is the most refined method that governments have for blocking Internet traffic. As mentioned above, deep packet inspectors examine not only a packet's header but also its payload. For instance, certain keywords can be both monitored and the e-mail containing them can be kept from reaching its intended destination.

This gives governments the ability to filter packets at a more surgical level than any of the other techniques discussed so far. While providing the most targeted traffic monitoring and shaping capabilities, DPI is also more complicated to run and is far more labor-intensive than other traffic-shaping technologies.

Appendix B. Technologies Used to Circumvent Censorship[66]

Each of the circumvention methods explained below can, in general, be considered an anonymous "proxy server." A proxy server is a computer system or an application program that acts as an intermediary for requests from a user seeking resources from other servers, allowing the user to block access to his or her identity and become anonymous.

Web-Based Circumvention Systems

Web-based circumvention systems are special web pages that allow users to submit a URL and have the web-based circumventor retrieve the requested web page. There is no connection between the user and the requested website as the circumventor transparently proxies the request allowing the user to browse blocked websites seamlessly. Since the web addresses of public circumventors are widely known, most Internet filtering applications already have these services on their block lists, as do many countries that filter at the national level.

Examples: Proxify, StupidCensorhip, CGIProxy, psiphon, Peacefire/ Circumventor.

Web and Application Tunneling Software

Tunneling encapsulates one form of traffic inside of other forms of traffic. Typically, insecure, unencrypted traffic is tunneled within an encrypted connection. The normal services on the user's computer are available, but run through the tunnel to the non-filtered computer which forwards the user's requests and their responses transparently. Users with contacts in a non-filtered country can set up private tunneling services while those without contacts can purchase commercial tunneling services. "Web" tunneling software restricts the tunneling to web traffic so that web browsers will function securely, but not other applications. "Application" tunneling software allows the user to tunnel multiple Internet applications, such as e-mail and instant messenger applications.

Examples: Web Tunneling: UltraReach, FreeGate, Anonymizer, Ghost Surf. Examples: Application Tunneling: GPass, HTTP Tunnel, Relakks, Guardster/SSH.

Anonymous Communications Systems

Anonymous technologies conceal a user's IP address from the server hosting the website visited by the user. Some, but not all, anonymous technologies conceal the user's IP address from the anonymizing service itself and encrypt the traffic between the user and the service. Since users of anonymous technologies make requests for web content through a proxy service, instead of to the server hosting the content directly, anonymous technologies can be a useful way to bypass Internet censorship. However, some anonymous technologies require users to download software and can be easily blocked by authorities.

Examples: Tor, JAP ANON, I2P

End Notes

[1] Freedom House is an independent watchdog organization that supports the expansion of freedom around the world. Freedom House supports democratic change, monitors freedom, and advocates for democracy and human rights. More information can be found on its website, http://www.freedomhouse.com.

[2] Danforth Austin, Director, Voice of America, testimony before the Subcommittee on Europe, House Committee on Foreign Affairs, Washington, July 23, 2009.

[3] Lucie Morillon, Washington Director of Reporters Without Borders, Testimony before the Tom Lantos Human Rights Commission, U.S. House of Representatives, Washington, June 18, 2009.

[4] Ibid.

[5] Ibid.

[6] Nicole Wong, Deputy General Counsel, Google, Inc., Testimony before the U.S. Senate Judiciary Committee's Subcommittee on Human Rights and the Law, Washington, May 20, 2008.

[7] Testimony of Mark Chandler, Cisco Systems, before the Senate Committee on the Judiciary Subcommittee on Human Rights and the Law, May 2, 2008.

[8] Testimony of Nicole Wong, Google, op. cit. May 2, 2008.

[9] See Reporters Without Borders, "Handbook for Bloggers and Cyber-Dissidents," http://www.rsf.org/IMG/pdf/ guide_gb_md-2.pdf.

[10] Prepared by Thomas Lum, Specialist in Asian Affairs, 7-7616.

[11] U.S. Department of State, 2008 *Human Rights Report: China*, February 25, 2009; PEN American Center, "Failing to Deliver: An Olympic-Year Report Card on Free Expression in China," July 8, 2008.

[12] Rebecca MacKinnon, "Bloggers and Censors: Chinese Media in the Internet Age," *China Studies Center*, May 18, 2007.

[13] Kim Zetter, "China Stands Firm in Response to Google Threat," *Wired*, January 14, 2010.

[14] Gillian Wong, "China Denies Involvement in Google Hackings," *Associated Press*, January 25, 2010.

[15] Some experts estimate that the PRC government has employed 30,000 "Internet police." "On the Wrong Side of Great Firewall of China," *New Zealand Herald*, November 27, 2007.

[16] David Bandurski, "China's Guerrilla War for the Web," *Far Eastern Economic Review*, Vol. 171, no. 5 (July/August 2008).

[17] Such software is available internally and through foreign sources, including the U.S. government.

[18] The Tom Lantos Human Rights Commission, "The State of Global Internet Freedom," June 18, 2009; U.S. Congress, Senate Committee on the Judiciary, Subcommittee on Human Rights and the Law, *Global Internet Freedom: Corporate Responsibility and the Rule of Law*, May 20, 2008. U.S. Congress, House Committee on International Relations, Subcommittee on Africa, Global Human Rights and International Operations and Subcommittee on Asia and the Pacific, *The Internet in China: A Tool For Freedom or Suppression?*, February 15, 2006.

[19] Cisco's general counsel argued that Cisco does not customize its equipment for China; filtering technologies that are intrinsic to Cisco products cannot feasibly be eliminated; Cisco has a written code of conduct that aims to prevent the modification of its products in foreign countries in such as way as to undermine human rights; and Cisco complies with all U.S. government regulations or export controls that restrict the sale of high tech products and crime detection equipment. See Anne Broache, "Senators Weigh New Laws over China Online Censorship," news.cnet.com, May 20, 2008; Mark Chandler, Cisco Systems, Testimony before the Senate Committee on the Judiciary, Subcommittee on Human Rights and the Law, May 20, 2008; Mark Chandler, Cisco Systems, Testimony before the Subcommittee on Africa, Global Human Rights and International Operations and the Subcommittee on Asia and the Pacific of the Committee on International Relations, February 15, 2006.

[20] "Isaac Mao and Michael Anti at Hong Kong U.," April 17, 2007, http://rconversation.blogs.com/rconversation/2007/ 04/isaac_mao_and_m.html.

[21] Peter S. Goodman, "Yahoo Says it gave China Internet Data," *Washington Post*, September 11, 2005.

[22] Christine Chiao, "Microsoft Erases Anti-Blog," *AsiaMedia*, January 17, 2006.

[23] Google's Chinese service, with roughly 80 million customers and 30 million Gmail accounts, has captured 20%-30% of the PRC market, compared to *Baidu*, which has over 60%. Tom Krazit, "Google's Censorship Struggles Continue in China," *news.cnet.com*, June 16, 2009; Steven Mufson, "China Faces Backlash from 'Netizens' if Google Leaves," *Washington Post*, January 13, 2010.

[24] Robert McMillan, "Google Moving Search Records Out of China," *InfoWorld*, March 1, 2006; Rory Cellan-Jones, "China and Google: What's Going On," *BBC – Dot.Life*, June 25, 2009; James Mulvenon, "The Rule of Law in China: Incremental Progress," *The China Balance Sheet in 2007 and Beyond*, Center for Strategic and International Studies, May 2007.

[25] Claudine Beaumont, "China Accuses Google of Spreading 'Vulgar Content,'" *Telegraph.co.uk*, June 25, 2009.

[26] "Google Apologizes to Chinese Writers," *Agence France Presse*, January 11, 2010.

[27] Jonathan Mirsky, "China's Tyranny Has the Best Hi-Tech Help Censoring the Internet," *International Herald Tribune*, January 16, 2006.

[28] Steven Mufson, "China Turning to Technology to Hold onto Power," *Washington Post*, April 16, 2006; U.S. Congress, "The Internet in China: A Tool for Freedom or Suppression?" op. cit.

[29] In January 2010, a U.S. software firm filed a lawsuit against the Chinese government for copyright infringement, unfair competition, and other legal violations in connection with the Green Dam program. Agence France-Presse, "U.S. Software Firm Sues Chinese Government for US$2.2 Billion," *South China Morning Post*, January 6, 2010.

[30] "Green Dam Launch 'Not Handled Well'," http://www.chinaview.cn, August 14, 2009.

[31] Rebecca MacKinnon, "China Tightens Internet Controls in the Name of Fighting Porn, Piracy, and Cybercrime," *Rconversation* , December 14, 2009, http://rconversation.blogs.com; Sharon LaFraniere, "China Imposes New Internet Controls," *New York Times*, December 18, 2009.

[32] *Rconversation*, October 10, 2009, http://rconversation.blogs china/ index.html.

[33] Estimates of the number of U.S. information technology, finance, defense, and other companies targeted in this attack ranged from 20 to 34.

[34] Google representatives stated that two Gmail accounts appeared to have been accessed but that the content of e-mail communications had not been breached. "Statement from Google: A New Approach to China," *Washington Post*, January 12, 2010. See also "A New Approach to China," *The Official Google Blog*, January 12, 2010, *http://googleblog.blogspot.com/* 2010/01/new-approach-to-china.html.

[35] Jessica E. Vascellaro and Aaron Back, "Fallout from Cyber Attack Spreads—Google Investigates China Employees; Rift Emerges Between Yahoo! and Alibaba," *Wall Street Journal*, January 19, 2010; Rebecca MacKinnon, "Google Puts Its Foot Down," *RConversation,* http://rconversation.blogs.com/rconversation/china/index.html, January 13, 2010.

[36] Miguel Helft, "For Google, A Threat to China with Little Revenue at Stake," *New York Times*, January 15, 2010.

[37] "Clinton Urges Global Internet Freedom," *VOA News.com*, January 21, 2010; Gillian Wong, "China Denies Involvement in Google Hackings," *Washington Post*, January 25, 2010; "China Says Google 'No Exception to Law'," Embassy of the People's Republic of China in the United States, January 19, 2010.

[38] Prepared by Casey Addis, Analyst in Middle Eastern Affairs, 7-0846.

[39] "ITU Internet Indicators 2008," International Telecommunications Union, *http://www.itu.int/ ITU-D/icteye/*Reporting/ShowReportFrame.aspx? ReportName= /WTI/ Information Technology Public&RP_intYear=2008& RP_intLanguageID=1.

[40] "Speed Reduced for High Speed Internet in Iran," *BBC Persian*, October 20, 2006.

[41] See the U.S. State Department "2008 Human Rights Report: Iran," *http://www.state.gov/g/drl/* rls/hrrpt/2008/nea/ 119115.htm.

[42] NSN is a joint venture between the Finnish cell phone maker Nokia and the German company Siemens.

[43] Stuart Smith, "Politics of Marketing: Why Brands Continue to Surf the Recession," *Marketing Week* (London), August 13, 2009.

[44] See Christopher Rhoads and Loretta Chao, "Iran's Web Spying Aided by Western Technology," *Wall Street Journal*, June 22, 2009.

[45] Nokia Siemens Networks, "Provision of Lawful Intercept Capability in Iran," June 22, 2009, http://www.nokiasiemensnetworks.com/press/press-releases/provision-lawful-intercept-capability-iran.

[46] Eli Lake, "Fed Contractor, Cell Phone Maker Sold Spy System to Iran," *Washington Times*, April 13, 2009.

[47] Prepared by Gina Stevens, Legislative Attorney, 7-2581.

[48] Deep Packet Inspection ("DPI") is a computer network packet filtering technique that involves the inspection of the contents of data packets as they are transmitted across the network.

[49] Many foreign countries have privacy laws that may be applicable to Internet Service Providers, websites, etc. See Morrison & Foerster's Privacy Library for the text of privacy laws in other countries, in the U.S., and for multinational organizations, http://www.mofoprivacy.com/ default.aspx?tabNum=2.

[50] See Andrew Noyes, "Chinese Demands for Web Filtering Software Cause a Stir," *CongressDailyAM*, June 25, 2009; Tim Wu, "The World Trade Law of Censorship and Internet Filtering," *Chi. J. Int'l L.*, vol. 7 (2006-07).

[51] Prepared by Kennon H. Nakamura, Analyst in Foreign Affairs, 7-9514.

[52] Under Secretary of State for Democracy and Global Affairs Paula Dobriansky, AOn-The-Record Briefing on the State Department=s *2006 Country Reports on Human Rights Practices,@* Washington, March 6, 2007, *http://www.state.gov/g/drl/rls/rm/* 2007/81468.htm.

[53] Ibid.

[54] U.S. Mission to the United Nations in Geneva, "Secretary of State Establishes New Global Internet Freedom Task Force," press release, February 14, 2006, http://geneva.usmission.gov/Press2006/02141InternetTaskForce.html.

[55] Secretary of State Hillary Rodham Clinton, "Remarks on Internet Freedom," January 21, 2010, http://www.state.gov/ secretary/rm/2010/01/135519.htm.

[56] On January 6, 1941, President Franklin Roosevelt addressed Congress saying that "we look forward to a world founded upon four essential human freedoms." These essential freedoms, which he referred to as the "Four Freedoms" are (1) freedom or speech and expression, (2) freedom of religion, (3) freedom from want, and (4) freedom from fear.

[57] The GIFT Strategy is available online at http://2001-2009.state.gov/g/drl/rls/78340.htm.

[58] Hillary Rodham Clinton, "Remarks on Internet Freedom," op. cit.

[59] Assistant Secretary of State for Democracy, Human Rights, and Labor Michael H. Posner, "Briefing on Internet Freedom and 21st Century Statecraft," January 22, 2010, http://www.state.gov/g/drl/rls/rm/2010/134306.htm.

[60] Questions following Secretary of State Hillary Clinton's *Remarks on Internet Freedom*, January 21, 2010, http://www.state.gov/secretary/rm/2010/01/135519.htm, and questions following Assistant Secretary of State Michael Posner's "Briefing on Internet Freedom and 21st Century Statecraft," January 22, 2010, http://it.tmcnet.com/news/2010/ 01/26/ 4590599.htm.

[61] Originally prepared by Gina Stevens, Legislative Attorney, 7-2581.

[62] See http://www.globalnetworkinitiative.org/.

[63] Legislative summaries are taken directly from the Legislative Information Service of the Library of Congress.

[64] This bill is a substitute for H.R. 4595.

[65] Prepared by Patricia Moloney Figliola, Specialist in Telecommunication and Internet Policy, 7-2508. Adapted from "The State of Iranian Communication: Manipulation and Circumvention," Morgan Sennhauser, Nedanet, July 2009, *http://iranarchive.openmsl.net/* SoIC-1.21.pdf; and "Five Technologies Iran is Using to Censor the Web," Brad Reed, Network World, July 2009, http://www.networkworld.com/news/2009/072009-iran-censorship-tools.html.

[66] Adapted from *Reporters Without Borders*, "Handbook for Bloggers and Cyber-Dissidents," September 2005, http://www.rsf.org/IMG/pdf/Bloggers_Handbook2.pdf; and *The Citizen Lab*, "Everyone's Guide to By-Passing Internet Censorship for Citizens Worldwide," University of Toronto, September 2007, http://citizenlab.org/Circ_guide.pdf.

In: Promoting Global Internet Freedom
Editor: Samantha R. Weber
ISBN: 978-1-61728-827-2

Chapter 2

OPENING STATEMENT OF SENATOR DICK DURBIN, CHAIRMAN, BEFORE THE SUBCOMMITTEE ON HUMAN RIGHTS AND THE LAW, HEARING ON "GLOBAL INTERNET FREEDOM: CORPORATE RESPONSIBILITY AND THE RULE OF LAW"

Dick Durbin

INTRODUCTION

This hearing of the Judiciary Committee's Subcommittee on Human Rights and the Law will come to order.

The subject of this hearing is "Global Internet Freedom: Corporate Responsibility and the Rule of Law."

After a few opening remarks, I will recognize Senator Coburn, the Subcommittee's Ranking Member, for an opening statement, and then we will turn to our witnesses.

There is a tendency to view human rights solely as a foreign policy issue. In this Subcommittee, we have learned that is an inaccurate perception. Our world is growing smaller every day, a process accelerated by the internet revolution.

We have seen that human rights violations in other countries can affect the United States. To take just one example, this Subcommittee has discovered that over a thousand war criminals from other countries have found safe haven in the United States.

On the flip side, the actions of the U.S. government and U.S. companies affect human rights in other countries.

In future hearings, we will explore the impact of Corporate America on other fundamental human rights, but today we will focus specifically on the role of U.S. technology companies in internet freedom around the world.

INTERNET FREEDOM AND CENSORSHIP

In 1791, the First Amendment of the Constitution was ratified, enshrining freedom of speech as the first fundamental right of all Americans. The First Amendment became an inspiration to people all over the world who yearn to throw off the yoke of oppression.

The year 2008 is the 60th anniversary of the Universal Declaration of Human Rights. After World War II, under Eleanor Roosevelt's leadership, the United States spearheaded the ratification of the Universal Declaration, which recognized freedom of expression as a fundamental right of all people.

The advent of the internet has allowed billions of people to exercise this right more fully.

However, the internet is not free for everyone. Contrary to early predictions that the internet could not be controlled, many countries censor the internet and jail online dissidents.

In Egypt, blogger Kareem Amer is serving a four-year prison term for entries on his blog relating to Islam and President Hosni Mubarak. Just last month, 27-year-old Esra Abdel Fattah was arrested after forming a group online to protest the high price of food in Egypt. She was released only in return for her promise to give up internet activism.

In Cuba, citizens can be jailed for using the internet for "counter-revolutionary purposes." Cuban Telecommunications Minister Ramiro Valdes said in February 2007 that the Internet was a "tool for global extermination."

In Burma last fall, the military junta imposed a black out on the internet when images of Buddhist monks protesting the military's rule started appearing online.

In China, dozens of bloggers have been jailed, including Hu Jia, who was recently sentenced to 3?? years in prison based in part on online essays he wrote criticizing the Chinese government's human rights record.

Over 30,000 internet police monitor the web in China and the so-called "Great Firewall of China" prevents Chinese citizens from receiving accurate information about China's human-rights record in Tibet and Darfur, among many other subjects. Animated "internet police" pop up periodically to remind users that the internet is monitored.

THE ROLE OF AMERICAN COMPANIES

In today's hearing, we will examine the role that American companies play in internet censorship. At the outset, let me acknowledge the obvious: this is not a black-and-white issue.

U.S. technology companies face difficult challenges when dealing with repressive governments. However, these companies have a moral obligation to protect freedom of expression, a fundamental human right that has enabled them to make billions of dollars. There is no question that they have fallen short of the mark on more than one occasion.

Human rights groups have accused Cisco of providing networking equipment that forms the backbone of the Great Firewall of China and is used by other repressive countries to censor the internet and monitor users. I want to note that late last week the Subcommittee received some troubling information about Cisco's activities in China. This information has been shared with Cisco and we will discuss this further today.

Software produced by American companies such as Fortinet and Secure Computing has allegedly been used to censor the internet in Burma and Iran, respectively.

Google received significant public criticism when it decided to launch Google.cn, a China-specific search site that removes results to conform with China's censorship policies.

At least 4 Chinese dissidents have been jailed based at least in part on information that Yahoo provided to the Chinese police.

Microsoft removes the blogs of internet activists from their blogging service in response to requests from repressive governments.

Internet Activism

Not all the news is negative, however. Around the world, internet activists are breaking down the walls of censorship. In Cuba, for example, students use flash drives, digital cameras, and clandestine internet connections to post blog entries and download information.

Yoani Sanchez, a Cuban blogger, poses as a tourist at internet cafes to make posts on her blog. She was recently named one of Time Magazine's most influential people of 2008.

Activists like Dr. Shiyu Zhou have also developed technology that allows users to break through firewalls and avoid censorship.

Three of our witnesses – Yahoo, Google, and Human Rights Watch – have been working for almost two years on developing a voluntary code of conduct for internet companies that do business in repressive countries. I look forward to hearing about the status of this long-awaited initiative. If American companies are unable to regulate themselves effectively, it may be time for Congress to step in.

Conclusion

As access to the internet continues to spread and change the way we inform and express ourselves, our government and American companies will be challenged to promote free speech and not to facilitate repression. With our collective efforts, perhaps someday the internet can fulfill its promise of empowering all people to exercise their right to seek information and express their opinions freely.

In: Promoting Global Internet Freedom
Editor: Samantha R. Weber
ISBN: 978-1-61728-827-2

Chapter 3

STATEMENT OF SENATOR TOM COBURN, M.D., BEFORE THE SUBCOMMITTEE ON HUMAN RIGHTS AND THE LAW, HEARING ON "GLOBAL INTERNET FREEDOM: CORPORATE RESPONSIBILITY AND THE RULE OF LAW"

Tom Coburn

I would like to thank Senator Durbin for holding yet another compelling hearing on issues affecting human rights and the law. Senator Durbin and his staff are truly to be commended for their dedication to issues of such heavy import. This relatively new subcommittee has proven to be quite a force, introducing bipartisan legislation to address genocide, human trafficking, and child soldiers. These bills are already well on the way to bringing justice to victims of the most egregious human rights abuses. The Genocide Accountability Act has already been signed into law, the Child Soldiers Accountability Act passed the Senate by UC, and the Trafficking in Persons Accountability Act awaits consideration by the full Senate after receiving unanimous approval of the Senate Judiciary Committee.

This kind of progress is unusual in today's partisan atmosphere, but Senator Durbin has ensured success by reaching across the aisle to work together to tackle these issues. Under his leadership, we have approached every issue objectively, studying issues closely and talking to experts both at hearings and behind the scenes. In so doing, we have developed reasonable proposals to close gaps in current law that have inadvertently allowed the United States to serve as a safe haven for human rights perpetrators.

Today we address the issue of internet freedom. Nearly one and a half billion people now use the Internet, 220 million of which reside in China. This number has more than doubled since early 2006, when the House of Representatives first held a hearing on this issue. Such growth is explosive, and, amazingly, China now has the largest Internet population in the world. The introduction and widespread use of this technology in countries like China is one of the most exciting developments of our day. Information is power, and the more that Chinese citizens access that information, the more open their society will inevitably be.

Of course, nobody understands the power of the Internet better than the governments who seek to repress those societies. I have already mentioned China, but that country is not the only government with such pernicious censorship. According to Reporters Without Borders, at least 62 cyber-dissidents are currently imprisoned worldwide, while more than 2,600 Web sites, blogs or discussions forums were closed or made inaccessible in 2007.

The group has identified countries where internet freedoms are restricted, which are: China, Cuba, North Korea, Belarus, Myanmar, Egypt, Ethiopia, Iran, Saudi Arabia, Syria, Tunisia, Turkmenistan, Uzbekistan, Vietnam and Zimbabwe. It named 11 additional countries as "countries under watch." It is my hope that today's hearing will shed light on how pervasive Internet censorship has become around the world.

This is not the first time Congress has addressed the issue of internet freedom. The House of Representatives, led by Congressman Chris Smith and the late Congressman Tom Lantos, held two recent hearings and have thereby created a thorough record for our benefit. I would like to thank my colleagues for their dedication to the issue and for the detailed groundwork they have already laid. The House hearings explored and established the factual record surrounding the relatively short history of American companies that have provided Internet service in countries where censorship is required by law. Those hearings examined in detail the steps and missteps of these companies as they began doing business in unfamiliar territory.

It is my hope that today we will tackle the challenge of discussing possible solutions for the problems that face these companies. While understanding the past is an important aspect of shaping solutions for the future, it is my hope that we can avoid re-litigating the same issues that have already been discussed at length. Our panel of witnesses, which includes industry experts and human rights advocates, should be able to explain the progress that has been made since the last hearing on this issue and answer questions that will help us better understand the challenge of preserving internet freedom around the world.

And while the focus of this hearing is worldwide, it is also my hope that while the eyes of the world are on China — in its response to the tragic earthquake and in anticipation of the summer Olympics — China's eyes are also on us, as we criticize government censorship of the Internet and call for more freedom for its citizens. I view this time as an opportunity to show the people of China what freedom looks like, and also to let the Chinese government know that its actions have not gone unnoticed. This is just another opportunity to lead by example, which is what I hope the American internet companies doing business in places like China will also choose to do. Their presence in these places is important, and it is crucial that they operate on the side of those seeking freedom, rather than oppression.

I look forward to the witnesses' testimony

In: Promoting Global Internet Freedom
Editor: Samantha R. Weber
ISBN: 978-1-61728-827-2

Chapter 4

TESTIMONY OF NICOLE WONG, DEPUTY GENERAL COUNSEL, GOOGLE, INC., BEFORE THE SUBCOMMITTEE ON HUMAN RIGHTS AND THE LAW, HEARING ON "GLOBAL INTERNET FREEDOM: CORPORATE RESPONSIBILITY AND THE RULE OF LAW"

Nicole Wong

Chairman Durbin, Ranking Member Coburn, members of the subcommittee.

Thank you for inviting me to discuss with you the issue of internet freedom and Google's efforts to maximize online freedom of expression and access to information. My name is Nicole Wong, and I'm Google's Deputy General Counsel. In that role, I am responsible for helping to address limits on free speech that Google faces around the world.

Google's commitment to freedom of expression is at the core of everything we do. Our company's mission is to organize the world's information and make it universally accessible and useful. We provide internet users with products like our search engine, Google Maps, and YouTube that let them quickly and easily share, receive, and organize digital information. In theory, any person – regardless of who she is or where she lives – can use these free products that enable free expression and information sharing.

The internet continues to be a powerful medium for propagating political opinions, religious views, and other core speech. And that trend has been accelerating. The estimated number of blogs has grown from fewer than two million in 2004 to more than 110 million this year. Expression through online video has become so popular that ten hours of videos are uploaded to YouTube every minute, and hundreds of millions of videos are watched on the site everyday. Even in countries where governments engage in heavy censorship, the internet has nevertheless proven to be an effective tool for sharing information and promoting political change.

However, the freedom of expression that's generated by blogs, social networks, video sharing sites, and other speech tools available on the internet is not embraced universally. As a global internet company operating in more than 150 countries – all with different national laws and cultural norms – we face daily challenges to our goal of making sure that the internet is a global platform for free expression.

With that in mind, I would like to make four main points in my testimony this morning: First, our products are above all else platforms for free expression and access to information.

Second, a wide range of legal and cultural barriers around the world regarding the free flow of information impact our products and services every day.

Third, we are working hard to respond to these challenges through policies and technology that promote free expression.

And finally, we believe that governments around the world can and must do more to effectively reduce internet censorship and promote free expression online.

GOOGLE'S PRODUCTS ARE OPEN PLATFORMS FOR FREE EXPRESSION

Most of our products – offerings like Blogger (our blogging service), Groups (our online bulletin board), orkut (our social networking site), Google Apps (our suite of collaborative productivity tools), and YouTube (our video sharing service) – are open platforms for free expression for which we do not generate the content. We do not serve as a gatekeeper and Google employees generally do not check content before it goes live, just as your phone company would not screen the content of your phone calls or your Internet Service Provider (ISP) would not edit your emails before you hit the "send" button.

Our products are often used as free expression tools in countries that restrict speech through other media. For example, in May 2007 Venezuelan President Hugo Chavez refused to renew the broadcast license of Venezuela's Radio Caracas Television on the grounds that RCTV violated broadcast laws, supported a failed coup against him in 2002, and more generally offered an anti-governmental perspective.

Despite protests by thousands in the streets of Caracas, the Venezuelan government replaced RCTV on May 28, 2007 with a state-run broadcast station. On that same day, RCTV's news department created a channel on YouTube on which it began airing daily installments of its newscast El Observador. Since then El Observador has been viewed more than 850,000 times, and many of RCTV's videos on YouTube have generated lively debates about freedom of expression. The inaugural post in response to the first El Observador video exclaims, "¡Viva la libertad de expresión!" (in English, "Long live freedom of expression!")

In other countries we have seen that communication platforms like internet video sites and blogs may be the only means for speech to emerge from communities closed off by authoritarian governments.

For example, when the military government of Myanmar (Burma) cracked down on protests by tens of thousands of Buddhist monks in the fall of 2007, it tried to do so outside of the public eye. During the protests, foreign journalists were kicked out, national media was shut down, and internet and cell phone service was disrupted within Myanmar in an effort to prevent information leaking out about the extent of the violence.

Nevertheless, tools like Blogger and YouTube were used by citizen journalists to share videos of the protests and information about the extent of the blackout, enabling the rest of the world to understand the human rights abuses taking place within the country.

As our Venezuela and Myanmar experiences indicate, our products are platforms for free expression, transparency, and accountability. Because of this, we often face efforts by governments throughout the world to restrict or deny access to our products.

Censorship Challenges that Google Faces

Most governments around the world have formal provisions for the protection of freedom of expression in their constitutions or fundamental laws. Indeed, the Universal Declaration of Human Rights, adopted by the United

Nations General Assembly in 1948, includes language that almost seems to have been written in anticipation of the borderless internet:

Everyone has the right to freedom of opinion and expression; this right includes freedom to hold opinions without interference and to seek, receive and impart information and ideas through any media and regardless of frontiers. [UDHR, Article 19]

Despite such formal undertakings, it is clear that many governments impose legal or practical limits on their citizens' freedom of speech. These limits on free expression take many forms. Some limitations are laudable and reflect shared moral imperatives such as the fight against child pornography. Others are rooted in culture and history, such as Thailand's laws against insult to the King, Germany's laws against Nazi propaganda, and India's laws against insulting religion or religious beliefs. And finally, of course, some governments, such as China, Iran, North Korea, Zimbabwe, and Myanmar, have imposed varying levels of political censorship.

Over the past several years, Google has encountered a wide array of governmental limitations to free expression online. Because our technologies and services enable every person with an internet connection to speak to a worldwide audience and, conversely, to read the words and watch the images posted beyond her nation's borders, Google has become a regular focus of governmental efforts to limit individual expression.

In my testimony today, I'd like to give you a sense of the scale and nature of these governmental efforts, and to explain how Google has attempted to promote freedom of speech while navigating the different governmental demands to limit access to information.

- YouTube: Since 2007, our YouTube video sharing site has been blocked in at least 11 countries including China, Thailand, Turkey, Pakistan, Morocco, Brazil, Syria, Indonesia, Iran, Saudi Arabia, and Myanmar.
- Blogger and Blog*Spot: In the last couple of years, we have received reports of our Blogger and Blog*Spot blogging sites being blocked in at least seven countries including China, Spain, India, Pakistan, Iran, Myanmar, and Ethiopia.
- orkut: Our social networking site, orkut, has been blocked recently in Saudi Arabia, Iran, and the United Arab Emirates.

Though we do not believe that it is ever justifiable for a country to block one of our services in its entirety, it is notable that the stated rationales for these instances of blocking range from relatively benign, apolitical, and culturally- and historically-driven content regulations all the way to heavy-handed political censorship directly contrary to basic international standards of political, religious, academic, and cultural freedom of expression.

To fill out this picture, here are three examples of government efforts to restrict expression that resulted in the outright blocking of YouTube for a period of time:

- Turkey and the Ataturk videos. YouTube has been blocked in Turkey repeatedly over the past year because of videos deemed insulting to Mustafa Kemal Ataturk, the founding father of modern Turkey, and other videos deemed by the Turkish government to be threatening to the state, such as videos promoting an independent Kurdistan. Under Article 301 of Turkish law, it is a crime to denigrate Turkishness, to threaten the unity of the Turkish state, or to defame Ataturk. As a result, Turkish courts have ordered the entire YouTube site blocked multiple times, and for several days, because of videos deemed illegal in Turkey. While we have been engaged with Turkish officials for many months, it has been very difficult to even know what videos have been the source of complaint.
- Indonesia and the "Fitna" film. Earlier this year, the controversial short film "Fitna" was uploaded to YouTube. Produced by a Danish politician, the film mixes clips of terrorist acts and propaganda and passages from the Koran to critique Islam in a manner offensive to some viewers. In Indonesia, high-level government officials publicly demanded that YouTube and other sites hosting the video immediately remove the content, in order to minimize the odds of violent protest riots. The government ordered Indonesian ISPs to block the entire YouTube site, preventing users within the country from viewing any videos. This had the ironic effect of blocking dozens and dozens of videos criticizing and responding to "Fitna" from Indonesians. We engaged in a dialog with the Indonesian government to determine what videos they objected to, and worked with local counsel to assess whether the videos violate Indonesian laws against hate speech. In the face of public pressure over the censorship and without further guidance from the government, Indonesian ISPs began lifting the site-wide block. It is our policy to only narrowly remove illegal content for the jurisdiction in which it is banned. As such, Google subsequently took steps to block the "Fitna"

video from being viewed within Indonesia due to its likely illegality, but kept it available to users in all other countries.

- China and YouTube. In October 2007, at a time when the Dalai Lama was awarded the Congressional Gold Medal and the Communist Party Congress convened in Beijing, YouTube was blocked throughout China. While we were not informed of the exact cause of this suppression of speech and we did not ourselves remove any videos from YouTube, access to the site in China was reinstated following the conclusion of the Party Congress.

As these examples indicate, despite our efforts to minimize restrictions on speech, we routinely face situations where governments attempt to limit expression through our products.

A broad range of global censorship efforts As noted above, some censorship efforts are relatively benign and stem from factors such as cultural sensitivities and history. For example, when reported to us, we remove links to content that promotes violence against protected groups from the search results for our Canadian search engine, Google.ca, because such content is illegal under Canada's Human Rights Law. On the other end of the spectrum are governments that prohibit commentary or criticism on certain political or otherwise sensitive topics.

Some of these efforts affect our global products; others affect a localized version of our products we have created to better serve a country market. For example, we have launched our search service in Spanish for Argentina. That service is located at www.google.com.ar, and because it is associated with Argentina's top level domain (".ar") and has various other links to Argentina, we apply Argentine law to our removal decisions. By contrast, we do not apply non-US law to the removals from our search service located at www.google.com.

Generally speaking, this distinction allows us to provide .com services with few restrictions on content and localized services with restrictions relevant to the local jurisdiction. The Google.ca example above is illustrative of this point. Another example is what we do in Germany, which bans the promotion of Nazism. German law makes Nazi content illegal, so we remove such content from our products hosted on our German domain, Google.de, when we become aware of such material. However, we do not remove Nazi content because of German law from our global products hosted on Google.com.

On a practical level, these different laws result in a variety of national standards on what can be restricted, which often poses difficult challenges for our services that can be accessed by a global audience. And these legal differences pose not only compliance difficulties but also real technical challenges. Restricting content that is perfectly legal in one country but illegal in another is not easily done on global internet services.

National governments often lack the technical ability and tools needed to address illegal content in a granular fashion, which often results in blocking access to a product as a whole, rather than just to a particular video or blog post. For example, earlier this year, Pakistani concern over an anti-Islamic video actually resulted in a global outage of YouTube after a national ISP erred in implementing orders by that government to block YouTube within the country. Global users of YouTube, including those in the U.S., were redirected to a non-existent site, and they were therefore unable to access the service for several hours.

THE CASE OF CHINA

China is a case that has posed for us all of the legal and technical hurdles described above, along with other challenges.

For several years prior to 2006, Google experienced widespread blocking of or other interference with our global search service, Google.com in China. To respond to this interference, in 2006 we launched Google.cn, a filtered search service that operates in China in conformity with local laws, regulations, and policies on illegal content. In doing so, and to provide transparency to our users in China, we became the first search engine in that country to post a notice on the search results page when certain links have been removed. Google.cn has not been subject to outright blockage.

Our Google.cn website supplements, and does not replace, our unfiltered (but periodically interrupted) Chinese-language interface on Google.com. Google.com remains open for Chinese-speaking users worldwide, including within China, when it is not being blocked by the government.

Let me stress that the decision to operate a filtered search engine at Google.cn was a difficult one. It was reached after more than a year of analysis and discussion by our senior management, and we continue to debate how to best operate in China.

The decision was based on a judgment that Google.cn would make a meaningful – though imperfect – contribution to the overall expansion of access to information in China. To date, we believe that on balance the decision to operate in China was the right one because our presence in China has led to improvements in freedom of expression.

For example, we believe that more internet users in China can access more information outside of China through Google.cn than through other offerings. In addition, our engagement in China through Google.cn has driven industry advances in transparency to users. Today, leading search engines in China, including the market leader Baidu, have followed our lead and now provide disclosures when they remove results. This was not the case before Google.cn established this practice with its launch in 2006.

Google's Response to Censorship Efforts

Google works to ensure that our products serve as platforms for free expression, and we are deeply committed to making sure that our products remain vehicles for individual speech, collaboration, learning, and political participation.

To realize these aspirations, we are engaged in numerous activities to help promote free expression online.

Promoting Transparency

Providing our users with transparency – an understanding of how our products work – is one of our core principles. In the context of government regulation of content, we try to provide transparency whenever we are required to remove content from our products.

To this end, when we remove content from our search results in response to a legal request, we send the request to Chilling Effects (www.chillingeffects.org), a joint project of the Electronic Frontier Foundation and several academic institutions including Harvard, Stanford, Berkeley, and the George Washington School of Law legal clinics, when we are able to do so legally. Chilling Effects posts the removal requests on its website, and we link to the publication of the complaint in place of the removed content. We are a leader in this level of transparency and the only major search engine to regularly and publicly disclose these removals.

In China, we take the following actions to promote transparency on the Google.cn search engine:

- First, whenever we offer censored results on our Google.cn search engine, we present clear notification on the results page to users. That notification states that, in accordance with local laws, regulations, and policies, we have not displayed all of the results in response to a query. In our view, there is value in letting our users in China know that the information that they searched for exists but cannot be made available because of limitations imposed by their government.
- Second, our Google.cn search engine sometimes shows results that, when clicked on, do not go anywhere because access to the destination site has been blocked. In those instances we show snippets of the blocked page so that, again, Chinese users can see that results have been limited by their government's actions.
- We also provide a link to Google.com on the Google.cn home page, so that Chinese users know that there is an unfiltered alternative – at least to the extent that it is not being blocked.

Providing transparency for users is important because it tells them that, though they may not be able to access information, that information does exist and can be accessed through other means. Transparency allows users to make informed decisions about the services they choose to use.

Establishing Best Practices

One company alone can have only limited impact. In testimony before the U.S. Congress in 2006, we said that we would work with other technology and telecommunications companies to develop shared principles that can serve as guidelines for doing business in countries that restrict access to internet content and information.

To this end, Google has played an active part in efforts by a group of companies, human rights organizations, socially responsible investors, and academics to produce a set of principles to guide the response of companies when faced with laws, regulations, and policies that threaten free expression and improper government requests for access to personal information.

Our group has been meeting for more than 18 months and, although it hasn't always been easy, we are optimistic that we will reach an agreement not only on a set of principles but also on ways to demonstrate that companies are putting those principles into practice. Google has taken this process extremely seriously, with our employees investing hundreds of hours and exploring these topics with the senior leadership of the company.

We believe that this effort is consistent with our own current practice of conducting risk assessments that consider the impact on free expression and other human rights of entering new markets or introducing new products into existing markets. Our assessments balance our mission to provide information to citizens around the world with a need to protect our users as well as the safety of our employees around the world.

Collaborating with the Human Rights Community

We also engage with human rights bloggers and other agents of free expression to help them use our products to promote more robust and more diverse speech online.

For example, we have worked with organizations such as Witness, Amnesty International, UNICEF, The Human Rights Foundation, The Equality and Human Rights Foundation, Human Rights First, and Human Rights Watch to start YouTube channels that give voice to human rights issues often ignored by the mainstream media. One of our human rights partners, Witness, uses videos to shed light on human rights abuses around the world.

You can see many of these organizations' channels and the videos they produce at a special human rights channel that we've created located at youtube.com/humanrightschannel. And we continue to underscore our commitment to human rights in our products themselves. For example, we have worked on several human rights projects with the United States Holocaust Museum. The museum's "World is Witness" project uses Google Earth and Blogger to document and map genocide and related crimes against humanity. The initial entries are from a recent Museum visit to Rwanda and the Democratic Republic of the Congo to learn about the legacies of Rwanda's 1994 genocide. And the museum's "Mapping the Holocaust" project uses

Google Earth to map key Holocaust sites with historic content from its collections, powerfully illustrating the enormous scope and impact of the Holocaust.

FIGHTING CENSORSHIP THROUGH TECHNOLOGY

Finally, we continue to provide resources to support the development of technology designed to combat internet censorship. For example, we provide platforms where people can host anti-censorship projects free of charge, much in the same way that YouTube hosts videos and Blogger hosts blogs. For example, the developers of Gladder, a Firefox browser extension that is used to counter censorship, use our Google Code platform to host their project. In addition, Google provides development resources to TOR (The Onion Router), an anonymizing program that allows individuals to get around internet censorship technologies.

SUPPORTING GOVERNMENT EFFORTS TO PROMOTE FREE EXPRESSION

Google's Support for free Expression Initiatives

Internet censorship is a real challenge, and not one that any particular industry – much less any single company – can tackle on its own. Efforts to promote freedom of expression and to limit the impact of censorship require both private and public sector engagement.

To that end, Google has encouraged the U.S. government to make combating internet censorship a top priority. We believe that government-sponsored censorship is one of the largest barriers to providing more information online and more access to internet-based services – with serious implications for trade and human rights. It is vital for the U.S. Departments of State and Commerce and the Office of the U.S. Trade Representative – in this and in future administrations – to make censorship a central element of our bilateral and multilateral agendas.

In that vein, we applaud the U.S. government's efforts to date to promote the free flow of information in our trade agreements. In addition, the Department of State has helped promote freedom of expression on the internet.

Among other things, the State Department has created the Global Internet Freedom Task Force, an internal departmental coordination group that addresses challenges to freedom of expression and the free flow of information on the internet. The State Department has been a strong advocate in United Nations summits and other forums for the right of all persons to create, access, utilize, and share information on the internet, subject only to limited restrictions for legitimate government purposes.

Google has been supportive of these efforts – but we believe that more must now be done.

Recommendations for combating global internet censorship

As we approach the 60th anniversary of the signing of the Universal Declaration of Human Rights, we believe governments that embrace free expression should do more to ensure that the world community respects free speech in cyberspace. International agreements designed to ensure free expression – no matter the particular medium – exist and have been ratified by the U.S. and many, many other countries. However, more can be done to make sure that these agreements are effective and enforced.

The Universal Declaration resulted in the International Covenant on Civil and Political Rights, a U.N. treaty that entered into force over 30 years ago and is commonly known as the ICCPR. The ICCPR very clearly protects freedom of expression: "Everyone shall have the right to freedom of expression . . . to seek, receive and impart information and ideas of all kinds" through any medium. Recent interpretations of the ICCPR make clear that the internet is covered under the agreement.

However, not enough has been done to ensure that the ICCPR truly protects free expression online. We also believe that the U.S. government could act more aggressively to promote online freedom of expression.

We offer the following suggestions as ways of building upon existing human rights mechanisms to reinforce America's and the international community's commitment to free expression throughout the world.

- Promote the universal ratification of the International Covenant. Not every country that has signed the ICCPR has fully embraced its obligations by ratifying it. Approximately 30 countries are not parties to the agreement including China, Cuba, and Saudi Arabia. We would strongly recommend that the U.S. renew diplomatic efforts to encourage these countries to ratify the covenant, and to file separate declarations under the treaty to consent to the Human Rights Committee's jurisdiction over complaints by States against other

States. We also believe that more governments – including the U.S. – should be encouraged to join the covenant's First Optional Protocol, which enables individuals to file complaints.

- Strengthen and enhance the State Department's Global Internet Freedom Taskforce. Much has been accomplished by the State Department's Global Internet Freedom Taskforce, but the initiative could be given increased prominence, authority, and funding. Increasing and enhancing the role of the taskforce could leave behind a strong legacy for the current Administration in the area of free expression online, and help ensure that promoting internet freedom is a central priority for the next Administration. Among other things, the agenda could be given increased prominence and authority by, for example, appointing an Ambassador-at-Large for Internet Freedom – which would be a position similar to the Ambassador-at-Large for International Religious Freedom.
- Support increased focus by the UN Human Rights Committee on Internet freedoms. In the area of internet censorship, the States Parties to the ICCPR could focus more attention on impediments to free expression online. For example, the Committee could issue a general comment addressing relevant articles in the Covenant and how they apply to internet restrictions.
- Ensure that countries that are parties to the Covenant submit human rights reports enabling international review. The ICCPR requires States Parties to submit periodic reports on compliance with their ICCPR obligations – generally every four years – to the Human Rights Committee, which conducts a detailed review and issues an assessment of treaty compliance. Many governments have not complied with this requirement, and the United States itself was out of compliance until it submitted a report in late 2005. The U.S., now having fully embraced its reporting obligations, should work to ensure that States Parties file their reports on compliance with the ICCPR in a timely fashion. This may need to involve offers of support for developing countries who are daunted by the effort involved in drafting the reports and submitting them for review, but we believe that this would be a worthwhile investment that would help protect human rights around the world.
- Strengthen individuals' ability to file complaints under the International Covenant. The ICCPR enables individuals to file complaints with the Human Rights Committee. We believe that the

governments that promote free expression could provide funding and other support to non-governmental organizations and other groups to assist individuals in filing such complaints, as well as increasing awareness among relevant populations of their rights under the ICCPR. In addition, participating governments could, through the U.N., provide additional funding that would enable the Committee to address more individual complaints in a timely way, as the Committee is now substantially underfunded.

- Explore methods of shining more light on violations of freedom of expression. We believe that more attention focused on instances of internet censorship will result in greater accountability and transparency and – ultimately – less censorship by governments. For these reasons we would urge the U.S. government to promote enhanced monitoring of instances of internet censorship by governments.
- Promote free expression as part of foreign aid. We believe that the U.S. government could use foreign aid and other programs to better promote ICCPR compliance and free expression on the internet. For instance, the government could incorporate internet freedom of expression into support for and assessments of good governance. In a related area, Google has already urged officials at the Millennium Challenge Corporation to incorporate internet censorship in measuring whether candidate countries have achieved criteria for democratic governance.

At the same time, we continue to urge governments to recognize that information restrictions on the internet have a trade dimension. We urge the U.S. government in particular to continue to use trade agreements and other trade tools to promote the free flow of information on the internet, and to seek binding commitments wherever possible.

The bottom line is that much, much more can be done by the U.S., and at the international level by countries that respect free expression online, to ensure that individuals, companies, and others can use the internet as the free and open platform that it was designed to be. We would be happy to assist the Subcommittee in exploring and helping to implement these and other expression-enhancing initiatives.

Conclusion

I would like to conclude by thanking Chairman Durbin, Ranking Member Coburn, and the other members of the Human Rights Subcommittee for helping to highlight the importance of the internet to free expression around the world. It is only with the attention and involvement of leaders like yourselves that we can make real progress in the effort to combat censorship throughout the world.

We look forward to continuing to inform you about our speech-expanding products, our efforts to promote free expression, and our recommendations for policy makers in this very important category of basic human rights.

In: Promoting Global Internet Freedom
Editor: Samantha R. Weber
ISBN: 978-1-61728-827-2

Chapter 5

OPENING STATEMENT OF MICHAEL SAMWAY, VICE-PRESIDENT & DEPUTY GENERAL COUNSEL FOR YAHOO! INC., BEFORE THE SUBCOMMITTEE ON HUMAN RIGHTS AND THE LAW, HEARING ON "GLOBAL INTERNET FREEDOM: CORPORATE RESPONSIBILITY AND THE RULE OF LAW"

Michael Samway

Chairman Durbin, Ranking Member Coburn, Members of the Subcommittee, my name is Michael Samway and I am Vice President and Deputy General Counsel at Yahoo! Inc. I also lead Yahoo!'s global human rights efforts. I appreciate the opportunity to testify before you today.

At Yahoo!, we are deeply committed to human rights and to being a leader among technology companies in this area. Our company was founded on the principle that promoting access to information can fundamentally improve people's lives and enhance their relationship with the world around them. In the period since Yahoo!'s creation in 1994, the power and ubiquity of the Internet has exceeded even our most far-reaching expectations.

The Internet has dramatically changed the way people obtain information, communicate with each other, engage in civic discourse, conduct business and more. Even in countries that restrict people's ability to communicate with one another or access information, people are still finding meaningful ways to engage online. Over the last week alone, we have seen just how important new communications technologies can be in places like China. Internet and cell phone resources have proven invaluable as government authorities and individuals contend with the aftermath of a devastating and enormously tragic earthquake in Sichuan province.

With the goal of bringing Yahoo!'s technological tools to people around the world, we embarked on a mission to expand our business globally in the late 1990s. As one of the first Internet companies to explore the Chinese market, we launched a service with the belief that providing the people of China with innovative tools to communicate, learn, and even publish their own views was one effective means to improve their way of life.

We were joined in this strategy of engagement by many in the United States Congress and in both Democratic and Republican administrations alike. With the sporadic pace of political progress in China as well as the need for companies there to adhere to local laws, we've also learned that expanding into emerging markets presents complex challenges that sometimes test even the important benefits of engagement itself.

While Yahoo! has not owned or had day-to-day control over Yahoo! China since 2005, we continue to be concerned about the challenges we faced in that market and will certainly face in other markets in the years to come.

Skeptics have questioned whether American Internet companies should engage in these countries at all. Yahoo! shares these concerns, and we have confronted these same questions about engagement in challenging markets. Yet, we continue to believe in the Internet's transformative power and, on balance, its constructive role in transmitting information to, from, and within these countries. And we are committed to doing our part through supporting individual and collective action.

Governments – because of their enormous leverage – have a vital role to play. To that end, we have asked the U.S. government to use its leverage – through trade relationships, bilateral and multilateral forums, and other diplomatic means – to create a global environment where Internet freedom is a priority and where people are no longer imprisoned for expressing their views online.

Our CEO Jerry Yang has met personally with senior State Department officials, and earlier this year wrote a letter to Secretary Rice urging the State

Department to redouble its efforts to secure the release of imprisoned Chinese dissidents. Secretary Rice subsequently raised this issue with senior Chinese officials, and since then we have seen Members of Congress echo this call for U.S. diplomatic leadership. We hope these efforts will both intensify and bear fruit. We are also taking steps on our own. Jerry Yang announced the Yahoo! Human Rights Fund in November 2007, as part of a broader effort to address human rights challenges in China and around the world. We have partnered with noted dissident and human rights activist Harry Wu, who is here with us today, and the Laogai Research Foundation to establish this fund. The Yahoo! Human Rights Fund will provide humanitarian and legal support to political dissidents who have been imprisoned for expressing their views online, as well as assistance for their families. A portion of the fund will also be used to support the Laogai Research Foundation's educational work to advance human rights.

In order to fuse our global business with responsible decision-making on human rights issues, we have also established the Yahoo! Business & Human Rights Program. A key pillar of this program is a formal assessment of the potential human rights impact of business plans we develop for new foreign markets. This assessment examines the human rights landscape in a country, evaluates potential challenges to free expression and privacy, and offers strategic approaches to protect the rights of our users through legal and operational structures, among other methods. Yahoo! then tailors its entry into the new market to minimize risks to human rights.

Because it is so difficult for just one company to create systemic change, Yahoo! has also been a committed participant in a broad-based global human rights dialogue. We are working with industry partners, academics, human rights groups, and socially responsible investors to develop a global code of conduct that will guide technology companies operating in challenging markets. At Yahoo!, we are eager to make this global code a reality in the near future.

As an industry pioneer, Yahoo! is proud to have explored new ideas and markets, helping drive the transformative power of the Internet. Just like others who have gone first, Yahoo! has also learned tough lessons about the challenges of doing business in nations with governments unlike our own. Yahoo! is working intensively and at the most senior levels in the company to set the highest standards for decision-making around human rights. The initiatives we pursue at Yahoo! are intended to protect the rights of our users, improve their lives, and make the extraordinary tools of the Internet safely and openly available to people around the world.

I appreciate the opportunity to tell you about these efforts to date and about our plans to continue pursuing a global leadership role in the field of human rights. I look forward to answering your questions. Thank you.

In: Promoting Global Internet Freedom
Editor: Samantha R. Weber
ISBN: 978-1-61728-827-2

Chapter 6

WRITTEN TESTIMONY OF ARVIND GANESAN, DIRECTOR, BUSINESS AND HUMAN RIGHTS PROGRAM, HUMAN RIGHTS WATCH, BEFORE THE SUBCOMMITTEE ON HUMAN RIGHTS AND THE LAW, HEARING ON "GLOBAL INTERNET FREEDOM: CORPORATE RESPONSIBILITY AND THE RULE OF LAW"

Arvind Ganesan

Mr. Chairman:

I welcome the opportunity to speak on the important matter of global internet freedom. I would also like to thank Senator Coburn, the ranking minority member of this Subcommittee. As someone who is from Oklahoma and whose family still lives there, I'm proud to say that my parents are thrilled at the prospect of delivering my testimony in front of one of their senators.

Human Rights Watch believes that the internet is a transformative force that can help open closed societies and provide the near-instantaneous flow of information to inform the public, mobilize for change, and ultimately hold institutions accountable. We have warned, however, that there is a real danger of a Virtual Curtain dividing the internet, much as the Iron Curtain did during the Cold War, because some governments fear the potential of the internet, want to control it and the companies that provide the services and products tied to it; and users fear the consequences of using it as a medium for openness and accountability.

Today, I would like to address three issues in relation to global internet freedom:

- The actions by some governments to restrict the flow of information and to punish individuals who exercise their right to free expression through this medium.
- The ongoing efforts by industry, nongovernmental organizations (NGOs), academics, and financial institutions to press for self-regulation to ensure that leading companies who provide internet technologies and services are not complicit in abuses or forced by governments to capitulate to their repressive demands.
- The prospects for government-led change and opportunities to ensure respect for human rights, particularly in regard to companies.

GOVERNMENTS

In 2006, the human rights problems related to the internet in China came to light through Congressional hearings; reports by Human Rights Watch, Amnesty International, and other NGOs; and the press. Through those revelations, the public learned that the US company Yahoo! had provided user information to Chinese authorities that led to the imprisonment of online activists for years. We also learned that US companies, including Google, Microsoft, and Yahoo!, censor their search engines in China, in anticipation of what Chinese censors expect and in addition to what the Chinese government's firewall prohibits.

However, China is not the only government that actively tries to suppress its critics in the virtual world. Since 2006, there are other examples, both of activists being intimidated or silenced for their efforts and of restrictions that governments impose on the internet by controlling both providers and users:

- Just two weeks ago, on May 7, 2008, Egyptian officials beat Ahmed Maher Ibrahim, a 27-year-old civil engineer. His crime? He used Facebook to support calls for a general strike on May 4, President

Mubarak's 80th birthday. Few people actually participated in the strike, but three days later, he was abducted by Egyptian officials in civilian clothes, beaten and insulted at New Cairo police station, then taken to the headquarters of the Interior Ministry's State Security Investigations (SSI) department where he was subjected to more beatings, and threatened that they would sodomize him with a broomstick. He was released without charges on the morning of May 8, but his captors asked him for the password to the Facebook group that he reportedly started, asked him about other participants in the group (whom he did not know), and threatened to beat him even more severely the next time SSI detained him.

- In Russia, Saava Terentev, a musician in a town a little over 600 miles east of Moscow, is being tried as an "extremist" because he spoke out about corruption in Russian law enforcement after reading a newspaper story about a newspaper being harassed by the authorities for reporting on corruption. He issued a harsh critique of corrupt police in a blog posting and an extremely offensive, but clearly ironic, "modest proposal" that they be burned in the public square. It was shortly deleted by the blog's owner, but now the authorities are prosecuting him for his sarcastic rant. We believe that this is the Russian government's first test case to try to use a law to restrict free speech on the internet. Additionally, the government has promulgated a decree that allows unfettered surveillance of the internet and other communications mediums without telling the user or the provider. But they do require the provider (potentially companies) to pay for the surveillance equipment. There are also some troubling proposals that are being circulated in the Duma. One is to regulate websites that receive more than 1,000 hits a day. Another is to separate the Russian internet from the rest of the world, along the lines of the Chinese firewall, so that the government could monitor content and shut down the link between the Russian internet and the rest of the world. Between those efforts and the attempts to go after bloggers it appears that the internet, which is perhaps one of the few open forums left in Russia, is now falling under government control.
- During its crackdown, following protests by monks, Burma's military junta shut down the country's internet connections to make sure no information got into the country and more importantly, that little information got out of the country. In total, the OpenNet initiative found that the junta blocked about 85 percent of e-mail service

providers and virtually all of political opposition and pro-democracy sites. Then, in late September 2007, the government apparently disconnected the main telecommunications lines in two cities to stop the flow of information. Some bloggers, however, used satellite and cellphone services. This is a chilling example of how far certain governments will go to stop the flow of information.

- The government of Syria regularly restricts the flow of information on the internet and will arrest individuals who post comments that the government deems too critical. Internet use in the country has exploded in the last few years and could be a crucial medium for the flow of information. However, Human Rights Watch has documented at least five cases since 2005 in which the government has arrested individuals because they posted comments critical of the government online, sent critical e-mails, or posted other information on the web. For example, on June 30, 2007, military intelligence arrested Tarek Biasi because he "went online and insulted security services." He was held incommunicado by the authorities and then sentenced to three years imprisonment on May 11, 2008, for "diminishing national feeling" and "weakening the national ethos." These are not the government's only tactics. Security services often force internet café owners to spy on their customers. In one case, an internet café owner filmed a customer who was sending comments and information to opposition websites outside of the country. On July 25, 2007, the government promulgated regulations that required all website owners to display the name and e-mail of the author of any article or comment on their website. This brazen regulation is clearly intended to chill critical speech by making it easier for the government to identify its critics online, particularly as anonymous postings have become a crucial means for individuals to avoid surveillance, or worse. Finally, the government also blocks websites, most notably those that are critical of the government, such as Arabic opposition newspapers' websites outside of the country.

These are just some of the cases around the world in which governments try to restrict the internet and silence users. What is clear is that government efforts to control the internet have multiplied around the world. While China has in many ways become the poster child for our efforts to stop censorship abuses, for other repressive governments such as those I have mentioned, China provides a model to be replicated. If that model is the ideal for internet repression, then the role of companies cannot be overlooked since they are clearly part of the Chinese government's efforts to censor the internet and obtain user information. As we have previously documented, Microsoft, Google, and Yahoo! censor their search engines in anticipation of what the Chinese government expects. Blogs have been shut down, and user information has been turned over to the government.

A Voluntary Code of Conduct

On January 17, 2007, leading companies including Yahoo!, Microsoft, Google, Vodafone, French Telcom, and Telia Senoria, along with human rights organizations (including Human Rights Watch, Amnesty International, Human Rights First, the Committee to Protect Journalists, Human Rights in China, Reporters without Borders, and the World Press Freedom Association), socially responsible investors, and academics, started on a process to develop a voluntary code of conduct and process of enforcement to try to curtail censorship and protect user information. We believe a system with three critical features could make a real difference in many censoring countries. These features are: a strong but reasonable code of conduct, an effective but not overly bureaucratic governance process, and independent monitoring of companies that sign on to ensure they actually take steps to curtail censorship and protect their users. Now, almost 18 months later, it would be great to tell you that a code is finalized and a system is in place to address these problems, but instead, we are still negotiating, and in the meantime, internet users are no safer, and censorship continues.

Not every company is in the same place nor is it fair to say companies don't care about human rights. After a high profile lawsuit by the families of jailed cyber dissidents, Yahoo! settled and has set up a fund to help cyberdissidents obtain legal aid. Google has used technologies like Google Earth to monitor some of the world's worst human rights crises, such as Darfur.

However, as laudable as those efforts might be, they do not address steps companies should take to ensure that their operations do not contribute to violations of human rights, such as censorship or the persecution of cyberdissidents. Some companies have been more aggressive, especially those that have faced the most controversy. Yahoo! has raised these issues with the Secretary of State, and some companies, such as Microsoft, have become more rigorous about censorship and the circumstances under which they will take down blogs.

Much more remains to be done. While companies have developed differently in regards to their human rights procedures, a voluntary industry initiative is only as strong as its weakest link. Without disclosing the details of discussions that are under the Chatham House rules, I can say that a fundamental problem is that some companies continue to be very resistant to the idea of independent monitoring, in particular to a system that would allow for an independent third party to assess: 1) whether companies have put policies into place that demonstrate a respect for freedom of expression and user privacy; 2) that those polices are diligently implemented; and 3) that their implementation is effective in curtailing these human rights problems. Unfortunately, we do not have such a system. Right now, the preferred option for companies is a system in which they will decide who the monitors are and what they will see, while companies implement those standards at a pace convenient to them.

In other words, companies will express support for human rights but also ask the public to basically trust them to do the right thing. There are several problems with that approach. First, this is exactly the situation that led to the problems we are trying to solve. Companies have already been opaque and exercised discretion over their actions, and to claim that the same approach will change things is dubious. For example, in China, Google and others choose what to censor. Even though Google and other companies now provide a disclaimer to notify users that censorship occurs, they still decide what to censor and whether they will even challenge the government's actions.

Second, it is difficult to point to a company within the voluntary standards process that has robust human rights policies and procedures in place more than two years after the problems in China were disclosed. Google, for example, has actively resisted such efforts. On May 8, Google's board voted down two shareholder proposals, including one sponsored by Amnesty International and the NYC Pension Funds, calling on the company to implement policies and procedures to protect human rights and another calling for a board committee on human rights. Sergey Brin, the company's co-founder, abstained from the vote and expressed support for human rights, but felt these proposals were not the appropriate way to approach the issue. What he did say was, "I think it makes sense to have a separate, a group of independent people in Google who meet regularly to discuss [these issues]." Frankly, that is not good enough.

Google's resistant stance and the lack of consensus on voluntary standards raise a fundamental question: What is holding up these corporations from finding an effective means of protecting user privacy and curtailing censorship? It can't be technical or technological challenges because industries like pharmaceuticals are very complex yet regulated. And in the case of internet companies, nobody is calling for a massive new bureaucracy like those that regulate other industries, just an agreement to be independently monitored.

Mr. Brin also recently defended Google's activities in China. "Google has a far superior track record than other search companies with respect to making information freely available," he said. This is a bold statement, but on what basis is he making it and what assurance is Google giving to the public to support this claim? Without some form of independent assessment of their activities, assertions like this simply are not credible.

A key purpose of our joint voluntary initiative is to provide the public with real assurance so that they can have confidence in companies or an industry that claims to oppose censorship and respect user privacy. After all, it will be the public and users who are the victims of censorship and whose information may be turned over to authorities. But that assurance is unlikely without meaningful oversight. A useful analogy is that of airlines. We would not accept that the best way to monitor airline safety is to allow airlines to do it themselves. Instead, we insist that someone else oversee them and are rightly critical of both the airlines and the monitors if they fall down on the job. Independent oversight is a critical component in protecting the public interest and it should be in the case of protecting freedom of expression and user privacy. Independent oversight is especially important with a medium and technologies that have the power to open societies, and because companies have already shown that they cannot or will not do it themselves.

Government Intervention

While we hope and plan to work towards an effective voluntary standard, it is unlikely that voluntary initiatives alone will be sufficient. A voluntary initiative will not apply to companies that do not join and it is difficult to see how it will get effectively implemented in countries where the government is very good at dividing and pressuring companies to capitulate to its demands, sometimes in exchange for access to a lucrative market. And most importantly, a voluntary initiative may be least effective in curtailing governments' efforts to obtain user information about cyberdissidents from companies, because a voluntary effort is not sufficient to stand up against the pressures a government can assert against companies.

For those and other reasons, we believe a regulatory approach is a necessary complement to a voluntary initiative. It would help to ensure that the playing field is level for human rights since rules would apply to far more companies than those who join a voluntary initiative; that there are meaningful consequences for companies who do not respect those standards; it would make it more difficult for governments to force companies into becoming complicit in human rights abuses; and could encourage a more assertive US foreign policy on these issues. There have been proposals circulating in Congress and one is in the House. We believe that any regulation should, at a minimum, contain the following elements:

- A requirement that companies have effective policies and procedures in place to safeguard human rights modeled after provisions in the US Foreign Corrupt Practices Act.
- A provision that requires companies to catalog and record efforts by governments to censor information.
- A process in which foreign government requests for user information can be referred to US diplomatic channels so that a company and its personnel are at less risk of pressure or retaliation.
- A requirement that companies locate personal information outside of jurisdictions that punish individuals exercising their right to free expression where the authorities may try to obtain personal data to do so.
- A private right of action so that victims can seek redress against companies that violate their rights.
- Clear and aggressive steps that the US government should take to combat censorship and protect user privacy through its foreign policy, trade policy, and other means.
- An examination of whether certain types of hardware and software, such as servers and other equipment, should be subject to export controls because of their capacity to be used by governments to spy on individuals and censor information.
- Effective penalties to deter companies from violating human rights.

- Restricting access to federal funds for companies that do not abide by these standards.

A useful model for this approach is the Foreign Corrupt Practices Act (FCPA). That act allows for companies to face penalties if they do not have adequate systems in place to prevent bribery as well as penalties if they actually engage in corruption. That approach could work quite well in regards to the internet and would easily complement a voluntary initiative since it would require a company to put systems into place to prevent abuses and would also hold it accountable were the company party to abuses. The FCPA also disproves the notion that regulations intended to protect the public good limit companies' ability to do business. The FCPA has been in force for more than 30 years and US business is still thriving abroad. Indeed, Microsoft, Google, and Yahoo! did not even exist when the act was passed, yet they seem to be doing reasonably well.

Companies have said that they might support regulation in theory, but seem to oppose existing efforts. Much like human rights policies and a voluntary initiative, they support them in principle, but apparently, not in practice. It would be helpful to understand how the companies and the industry intend to move forward effectively and credibly in terms of voluntary and mandatory standards. I would welcome the opportunity to come before you again or at regular intervals to report on such progress and would hope that the other witnesses today would do the same.

Thank you again for this opportunity to speak on this important subject.

In: Promoting Global Internet Freedom
Editor: Samantha R. Weber
ISBN: 978-1-61728-827-2

Chapter 7

TESTIMONY OF MARK CHANDLER, SENIOR VICE PRESIDENT LEGAL SERVICES, GENERAL COUNSEL AND SECRETARY, CISCO SYSTEMS, INC., BEFORE THE SUBCOMMITTEE ON HUMAN RIGHTS AND THE LAW, HEARING ON "GLOBAL INTERNET FREEDOM: CORPORATE RESPONSIBILITY AND THE RULE OF LAW"

Mark Chandler

Mr. Chairman, Members of the Subcommittee:

My name is Mark Chandler, Senior Vice President and General Counsel of Cisco. Thank you for the opportunity to address some very important and difficult issues that speak directly to the future of the Internet.

First, I'd like to share with you some background about the products our company is best known for. Networking equipment - routers and switches - forms the core of the global Internet and most corporate and government networks. Cisco has often been described as the "plumbers" of the Internet, as our technology constitutes the "pipes" that connect one location to another. Originally our products were designed for communications within private or corporate networks. When the public Internet emerged in the mid '90s, our products found immediate application for worldwide use. We now have many competitors around the world who build products that perform similar functions. When you send an email in your office to your children or grandchildren, the digital language that makes up that email is routed through equipment made by Cisco or our competitors

Over the last year, we have seen remarkable growth and transformation related to the Internet. The Internet continues to expand around the world and new applications such as collaboration tools and the use of video are transforming how we work, live, play and learn. More than 1.4 billion people now use the Internet, an increase of 300 million people in just one year. And new mobile devices such as the Apple iPhone have enabled millions of people to do what they want, when they want, with whom they want.

But at the same time, we have observed some troubling events and challenges related to the manipulation of Internet technology. Later this month will be the first anniversary of an unprecedented cyber attack that crippled the Estonian government and commercial networks. The attacks were labeled "cyber terrorism" and prompted NATO to create a new multi-national initiative to prevent such incidents. And in February, an ISP in Pakistan caused an international incident when it rerouted its computers to block YouTube from being watched in the country. The act had much broader implications by effectively hijacking the site for several hours worldwide. These incidents demonstrated that despite the Internet's redundant nature, it can still be disrupted by unilateral actions and by cyberattacks. Every major corporate and service provider network is subject to nearly constant attack.

Attacks can take many forms, some of which are referred to as worms, viruses, denial of service attacks, and more. Network management and security capabilities are essential to mitigate attacks and thus enable information flow. No network can be administered by our customers without the ability to manage and protect the information that flows through it. Without this capability, it would not be possible to operate the Internet and the Internet would likely not exist as it does today. For example, without these tools, the Government of Estonia would have been powerless against the attacks it faced last year.

These tools are essential for many reasons. But the technology that is used to manage and protect against hackers or viruses is the same generic technology that filter or control Internet access by children, or the illegal downloading of copyrighted material. If, for example, a network administrator knows that a certain website is dangerous to her network because a virus or spyware has been downloaded from that site, or because the site is pornographic, she can use IP address blocking (each website and user on the Internet has an IP — Internet Protocol — address - the equivalent of a phone number) to protect her network from that site. This technology is a customary part of network management software of all major suppliers of Internet equipment -- Cisco's and our competitors' -- and is basic to network functionality. Whether for security or the management of information, the technology is one and the same. The filtering that occurs is implemented by the owner or administrator of the network using technology that is available regardless of the manufacturer.

In no country has the issue of the Internet and how it should be managed been more prominent than in China. China now has the largest Internet population in the world with 220 million users. There is no question that the Internet has been good for China and its people. It has provided unprecedented access to information. It's transforming China and its economy and it's helping the Chinese people engage more with the world.

Perhaps the most vivid example of the dramatic changes the Internet has brought to China is the response to last week's earthquake in the southwest region of the country. With mobile communications systems down or damaged, the Internet became a critical source of information for family and loved ones, as well as the rest of the world. Within minutes, pictures and videos from the region were online. That stands in stark contrast to the events in Tangshan 32 years ago, when the world received no official confirmation for months that a 7.8 magnitude earthquake had even happened, despite the deaths of an estimated 240,000 people and the destruction of much of that region.

As a company that supports free expression and open communication on the Internet, and believes that its products inexorably drive the world toward more open communication, Cisco respects the strength of conviction of those who bring concerns forward about efforts of various governments to censor freedom of expression on the Internet and persecute those who attempt to use the Internet for purposes of political speech. But we also must respond when Cisco is erroneously linked with these efforts.

To set the record straight, it is important that the Committee understand that Cisco does not customize, or develop specialized or unique filtering capabilities, in order to enable different regimes to block access to information. Furthermore, Cisco sells the same equipment worldwide. Finally, Cisco is not a service or content provider, nor are we a network manager. Allegations that Cisco has built a "great firewall" in China or elsewhere confuse the provision of the basic pipes of the Internet, which include J,asic security features that every network must have, with more specific technological mechanisms which may be implemented to achieve the invasive effects that have raised specific concerns.

Some countries have chosen to restrict or limit access to information on the Internet based on political considerations, rather than on the freedoms that we enjoy in this country. While many have commented on the activities of the Chinese government in this regard, the issue is, in fact, global. Some Middle Eastern countries, for example, block sites critical of their leadership. And judicial action has been taken in France due to the failure of an operator to block local users' access to some types of information.

Cisco, however, has not and does not design products to accommodate political censorship. The tools built into our products that enable site filtering are the same the world over, whether sold to governments, companies or network operators. The features in our equipment are "off the shelf' and not altered in any way for any market or region. Similar technology is available from at least a dozen other US, Canadian, European and Chinese companies. Because of the threats to network operations that I previously mentioned, which exist around the world, there is no feasible way to manufacture equipment without these capabilities and it would not be desirable or sensible to do so. The management of information flow by a customer cannot be prevented by Cisco unless we are to also prevent the originally intended use of this technology, which would expose the Internet to the full risks of inevitable daily attacks. Networks attached to the Internet would literally stop working.

Cisco *does*, however, comply with all U.S. Government regulations which prohibit the sale of our products to certain destinations, or to certain users or to those who resell to prohibited users. We have not sold and do not sell our equipment to the countries listed on the U.S. Department of Treasury's OFAC (Office of Foreign Assets Control) list of embargoed nations, and we comply fully with all aspects of the Foreign Relations Authorization Act passed by Congress in the wake of Tiananmen Square.

More broadly, Cisco has played a leading role in helping to make Internet technology ubiquitous, allowing hundreds of millions of people in nearly every nation around the world to access information and ideas previously unavailable or inaccessible. Because our products are designed to expand the reach of communications systems, we build to open, global standards, and we vigorously oppose attempts by certain governments to balkanize the Internet by setting country-specific security requirements. We do not design custom or closed Internet systems. The Internet technology may not be perfect -and the Internet itself can be misused -- but there has been no greater force in spreading the power of ideas than the single worldwide Internet. The key to its growth and the flow of information it enables has been the standardization of one global network. This has been and remains the core of Cisco's mission.

For some, the Internet is a tool that liberates individuals from the constraints of time and distance, empowering those who previously had no access to the world's store of infoimation. Some are fearful of this liberation as a mechanism for empowering non- state actors. Still others see the Internet as a tool used by governments to control content.

The policy response is complex. Among the questions that we have historically raised are: Has the Internet helped promote a dramatic increase in access to information in regions where content is nonetheless subject to certain limitations? Does active public engagement in such countries help to influence policy decisions? What policies will best help constrain political and other censorship contrary to First Amendment principles? If countries that engage in censorship are to be denied U.S. Internet technology, will those countries establish closed-standard Internets of their own to further restrict access to information?

To that end, policies that encourage governments to build their own Internets could be highly counter-productive by removing the leading platform for free expression. At the same time, Cisco sees benefit in the U.S. Government in making freedom of expression an integral part of its diplomacy. One means to do that that has been proposed is through the creation of an Office of Global Internet Freedom within the International Broadcasting Bureau. In doing so, the U.S. Government would be unambiguous about its intentions.

When the Internet first became a societal tool, it was largely available in western countries with broadly shared viewpoints about freedom of expression. It is inevitable as the Internet grows globally that there are differing viewpoints about its role in society. That has been true of every transformational technology, for example the television in the 20th Century.

Our challenge going forward is to ensure that as the Internet is globalized, we don't let it be balkanized in a way contrary to our goal of expanding its reach and liberating power.

Thank you for inviting us to appear before you today.

In: Promoting Global Internet Freedom
Editor: Samantha R. Weber
ISBN: 978-1-61728-827-2

Chapter 8

TESTIMONY OF SHIYU ZHOU, PH.D., DEPUTY DIRECTOR, GLOBAL INTERNET FREEDOM CONSORTIUM, BEFORE THE SUBCOMMITTEE ON HUMAN RIGHTS AND THE LAW, HEARING ON "GLOBAL INTERNET FREEDOM: CORPORATE RESPONSIBILITY AND THE RULE OF LAW"

Shiyu Zhou

Mr. Chairman, members of the Committee, Ladies and Gentlemen. I would like to thank you for this opportunity to testify before you today on the topic of global Internet freedom and the Corporate Responsibility and the Rule of Law.

The lack of information freedom in closed societies is usually coupled with severe violations of human rights and it also puts the United States at risk. In Iran, Cuba and certain other totalitarian countries, information control is often used for manipulation and indoctrination and whipping up anti-US sentiment, as illustrated by the xenophobia fostered online in the People's Republic of China (PRC) following the Tibet crackdown and the Olympics Torch Relay. Violence begins with hate, and hate begins with distorted information.

Information control can also cost lives. When the PRC leadership chose to suppress news of the SARS outbreak in 2002, the virus spread far beyond China's borders to places like San Francisco, causing the death of at least several hundred victims and almost a global pandemic.

The Internet has become the greatest hope for global information freedom. It is a vast, fast, and inexpensive way to access information and to communicate and the number of Internet users worldwide has soared. By January of this year, the PRC had 210 million users and has since surpassed the US, and both Iran and Vietnam were at 18 million users and growing. While authorities in closed societies can easily shut down newspapers, block TV channels, jam short-wave radios, and ban books, the Internet is far more elusive. With the proper anti-censorship technologies, users in these societies can access uncensored information online freely and without fear of reprisal. Anti-censorship is sometimes called anti-blocking or anti-jamming and refers to technical means that protect users in closed societies from being monitored, blocked, or tracked.

For more and more users around the world, that proper anti-censorship technology means tools like FreeGate and UltraSurf -- created by the Global Internet Freedom Consortium (GIF), a small team of dedicated men and women, connected through their common practice of Falun Gong, who have come together to battle tens of thousands of Internet monitors and censors around the world to work for the cause of Internet freedom. I am proud to stand before you today on behalf of this illustrious group because I feel they are truly heroic. They have allowed millions of citizens inside repressive societies to experience the Internet as we in free societies experience it – being able to use Wikipedia to look up a new word or post a blog without having to look over their shoulders. The Consortium provides its products and support services to those citizens entirely free of charge.

The companies and organizations that make up the Consortium have maintained the world's largest anti-censorship operation since 2000. The focus was originally on the PRC as China's censorship measures on the Internet are by far the most sophisticated and extensive among all the closed societies. As more and more nations have followed China's lead, however, our experience has made us uniquely equipped to help advance Internet freedom around the globe. Outside of China, the second largest segment of our user base is now in the Middle East: in Iran, Saudi Arabia, United Arab Emirates, and Syria.

Of the 43 countries identified as "Not Free" in Freedom House's Freedom of the Press 2008 Survey, GIF's anti-censorship systems have served users in the following 33 countries as of January 2008: Algeria, Angola, Azerbaijan,

Belarus, Brunei, Burma, Cambodia, Cameroon, China, Congo, Cote d'Ivoire, Cuba, Egypt, Iran, Iraq, Kazakhstan, Laos, Libya, Maldives, Oman, Pakistan, Qatar, Russia, Rwanda, Saudi Arabia, Sudan, Syria, Tunisia, United Arab Emirates, Uzbekistan, Vietnam, and Zimbabwe.

Our five existing tools – UltraSurf, DynaWeb FreeGate, Garden, GPass, and FirePhoenix — currently accommodate an estimated 95% of the total anti-censorship traffic in closed societies around the world, and are used DAILY by millions of users. These tools have been of benefit to US-based organizations such as Human Rights In China, the Chinese Democracy Party, Voice of America, and Radio Free Asia -- and even companies like Google and Yahoo since we bring the uncensored version of their services into closed societies like China.

As of January 2008, the Top Five censoring countries with the most average daily hits to our anti-censorship systems are (hits per day):

(a) China: 194.4 million
(b) Iran: 74.8 million
(c) Saudi Arabia: 8.4 million
(d) UAE: 8 million
(e) Syria: 2.8 million

Clearly, besides China, a significant portion of the user base is from the Middle East.

We have witnessed first-hand the effectiveness of anti-censorship technologies in improving information freedom for people in closed societies. During the democratic movement in Burma in late August 2007, our anti-censorship portals were receiving over 120,000 average hits from IP addresses originating inside Burma every day; a three-fold increase from less than 40,000 prior. That number has since more than doubled in the wake of the cyclone.

After the protests broke out in Tibet on March 10 of this year, there was a four-fold increase in the number of daily hits to our anti-censorship portals from Tibet, from the daily average of 120,000 before March 10 to about 480,000 after March 10. The daily number of hits reached more than 800,000 on March 16. The measures Chinese authorities have taken to clamp down on information going in and out of Tibet are severe. The Consortium's anti-censorship tools are now one of the Tibetans' few remaining links to the outside world.

A particularly insidious aspect to information control is that it allows a repressive government to spoon feed the populace with whatever false information it chooses. In closed societies such as China and Iran, censorship is used by the leadership to save face, deflect criticism, and turn domestic discontent against external enemies both real and imagined. A few carefully edited TV news segments, a few doctored articles in the newspapers, a few carefully placed key words to dehumanize the target, and the result is a very large and very hostile population. The US would do well to heed the very real threat this poses to our national security.

Internet freedom is one of the most effective ways to allow the US to win the hearts of the people in closed societies, and its young people in particular, and to help move the world in more benign and realistic directions. Anti-censorship technology can allow the people in closed societies to be better informed and to be less subject to manipulation by an unscrupulous leadership. Winning people over to a more open and free system via the Internet could very well be a way to avoid damage and loss of life in future conflicts. It is no exaggeration to say that an online information battle, if fought well, could ultimately help to prevent a real war.

It is thus not surprising that China maintains an Internet "firewall" bureaucracy of over 30,000 officials and that, as reported by the State Department/Foreign Operations Appropriations Committees, Chinese President Hu Jintao has spoken of a crisis involving "the stability of the socialist state" that will only be cured if the Internet can be "purified."

In the on-going struggle between the censors and anti-censorship efforts, it is crucially important to stay ahead of the game. Repressive regimes have been spending enormous sums on developing censorship tools in recent years. We should also be aware that China's military is actively developing sophisticated ways to wage digital warfare against America. For years, Chinese authorities have indoctrinated "patriotic hackers" to infiltrate and take down US government computer systems. Just recently, these hackers were instigated to attack the CNN website en masse. If the US does not maintain its current lead in anti-censorship technologies over censors now, there could be a much higher price to pay down the road.

Our statistical data show that currently Chinese elites are among the most avid users of our anti-censorship services, for they want to know what is happening in the world that their government does not provide them. It has been transforming the Chinese society in a peaceful but powerful way that must not be underestimated. Once a critical mass, 10 percent we believe, of the 230 million Internet users in China get to know the existence of our anti-censorship tools and, especially, gain a positive experience of using them, the avalanche effect of such a development will in our view lead to the fall of the Beijing censorship Wall and, consequently, to the fall of other Walls in the world's other closed societies. Imagine, then, the possibilities of the Pope being able to conduct an interactive worship service with millions of House Church Chinese Catholics, or Members of this Committee being able to conduct seminars in democracy with tens of thousands of Iranian students -- all without fear of detection or arrest using our scaled-up services.

The battle of Internet freedom is now boiling down to the battle of resources. It is our belief that $50 million – enough to allow GIF programs to scale up their operations through purchasing equipment and expanding network capacity - will be enough for us to reach the critical mass of 10 percent of the 230 million Internet users in China. Importantly, the time for doing so is this coming year, given the current political dynamic in China and the upcoming Olympics. We hope and trust the Senate and the Congress will grasp what we believe to be a historic opportunity.

Only when the US shows more determination to keep the Internet open than the closed societies are showing to seal it off, can there be the hope of information freedom and democracy for the citizens in all closed societies, and a more peaceful tomorrow for mankind.

We would like to thank Senator Leahy, Senator McConnell, Senator Gregg, Congresswoman Lowey, Congresswoman Ros-Lehtinen, Congressman Wolf, Congressman Berman, and other members of Congress, and Ambassador Mark Palmer of Freedom House, Michael Horowitz of Hudson Institute, former Director of NTIA Clay Whitehead, and Human Rights Watch DC Office Head Tom Malinowski, for the support they have provided my colleagues. In particular, we thank Senator Leahy, Senator McConnell, Senator Gregg, Congresswoman Lowey, and Congressman Wolf, for the Internet freedom initiative in the fiscal year 2008 Foreign Operations Appropriations Bill which set up a competition for a $15 million grant for "field-tested" Internet technology programs and protocols that, in the words of the appropriation legislation, "have the capacity to support large numbers of users simultaneously in a hostile internet environment."

Below is a more detailed description of the current state of Internet censorship around the world, how people have benefited from the services we've been providing, and how our services might be expanded to successfully tear down Firewalls in closed societies around the world.

THE STATE OF INTERNET CENSORSHIP

A number of countries actively censor the Internet, including Iran, the People's Republic of China, Burma, Saudi Arabia, and Vietnam. Since China's censorship measures on the Internet are by far the most sophisticated and extensive and are emulated by many other nations, the state of Internet censorship in China illustrates well the nature of the problem in other closed societies.

Since 1999, we have seen China's Internet censorship capability evolve from rudimentary measures to systematic and highly advanced technological deployments. Those of us who have worked for the world's top technology companies can tell that the capability and sophistication of the Chinese government's censorship technology is at such a level that they are using the most top-of-the-line, cutting-edge products.

Today there are three mechanisms at work on the Great Firewall. One is Internet Protocol Address blocking, or IP address blocking. An IP address on the web is like a phone number on a telephone network. IP address blocking is simply denying your visit to overseas websites with certain IP addresses. The websites targeted by the censors are mostly about Falun Gong, the Tiananmen Square massacre, Tibet, Taiwan, human rights, etc.

The second mechanism is called content filtering. Chinese authorities have built powerful net machinery to sniff all the net traffic going through the Great Firewall in either direction. Once they detect a keyword in the traffic, they will simply cut off that particular traffic flow. The user ends up staring at a blank screen as though he has suddenly lost his Internet connection. This method indiscriminately blocks access to any site that happens to have one of the keywords included on the long official list.

The third mechanism is the most malicious – we call it Domain Name Redirect. This method can be likened to publishing a phone book with the number of the people you dislike changed to other numbers so no one will ever be able to reach these people. Another analogy would be changing all the street signs so no one knows where they are actually going. This is a flagrant violation of international Internet conventions and standards on a national-scale, but apparently the censors do not feel any obligation to play by the rules when they want to control information.

Besides the technological aspect, there is a whole other dimension to censorship on the Net. We call it the "human flesh Great Firewall." At the top is an army of tens of thousands of net police patrolling the web space in China.

Down below are countless website administrators who are forced to sift through the blogs, forums, and bulletin boards they are managing to delete any posts deemed "sensitive" according to certain arbitrary rules. In addition, Internet service providers (ISPs) are told to keep an eye on the sites they are hosting and be ready to shut down the sites that cross another arbitrary line drawn by the state. Internet content providers such as search engines and portal sites also devote significant time and effort in preemptive self-censorship.

DEMAND AND IMPACT OF ANTI-CENSORSHIP SERVICES

Since the early days of the censorship, we have been providing censorship-circumvention service to users living in oppressive regimes. We started as a few independent and scattered groups, including Dynamic Internet Technology, Inc. (DIT), UltraReach Internet Corporation, Garden Networks for Freedom of Information Inc., World's Gate, Inc., and Global Information Freedom, Inc. Each group had a different technical approach.

Our services were originally targeted towards and promoted to Internet users in China, but over time we have also attracted a large number of users from other closed societies, such as Iran, Burma, and Saudi Arabia.

In 2006, these groups formed a consortium, Global Information Freedom Consortium to pool their experience, infrastructure, resources, and technological talents together. The purpose was to provide better service to users and beat censorship more effectively, especially when each of the groups had limited resources.

Our anti-censorship services were developed and evolved in response to two major user demands: to surf the web freely and securely and to post information on the websites inside China without exposing the identity and origin of the connection. Our services have three major facets:

1. Anti-censorship tools: These are a variety of software tools we provide to users to defeat blocking, monitoring and tracing of their online information and activities. When a user in China fires up our system, the bits and bytes flowing in and out of his/her computer are scrambled, so the Great Firewall cannot see any patterns in the traffic and therefore has no idea if it detects something suspicious or not. Additionally, our tools are highly dynamic and know where the cracks

in the Great Firewall are. The tool changes its network connection from time to time to avoid becoming a sitting duck.

Currently we have five major tools from our coalition to cater to our users' demands, including DIT's FreeGate, UltraReach's UltraSurf, Garden Networks' Garden, and World's Gate's GPass and FirePhoenix. They have different features and technical strengths and they are also constantly evolving in response to the ever-changing censorship technologies.

The variety of our tools provides our users with a real edge. They have reported that with such a selection, they are almost unstoppable. Whenever one of our tools is jammed by the censors, a user can switch to another tool to either get back online or download a newer version of the jammed one. Such a complementary nature seems to greatly enhance the users' confidence in our offerings.

2. Infrastructure: Once a user launches one of our tools, information is relayed to a network we have built in free countries, mostly in the U.S. This network is like an Underground Railroad in cyberspace, but much more dynamic. The capacity of this infrastructure directly impacts the number of users we can support.

   This network also provides extra services. For example, World's Gate provides low-cost web-hosting services to users in closed societies so they can enjoy freedom of expression by establishing forums, discussion groups, etc. on our network in addition to the native support of censorship-resistance.

3. Promotion and user support: We have found it is critical to perform user outreach, because the news about the availability of our services is itself blocked. Therefore we have to actively spread the word via the Internet using emails, instant messages, forum posts, and traditional means such as long-distance telephone calls and postal mail. Once the user base reaches a critical mass, it becomes much easier because the news can be spread through word-of-mouth.

Timely technical support for users is a must for a successful anti-censorship system. Our five systems (FreeGate, UltraSurf, Garden, GPass and FirePhoenix) are now sharing a unified technical support platform, www.qxbbs.org, in which each system has its own user forum. It is a place where users can share their experiences and developers can provide technical support. For example, there are more than 20,000 posts on DynaWeb's support forum with information ranging from technical tips to compliments from users to reports from China of new blocking test results. This operational area also includes internationalization, i.e., translation of user interface, documentation and instructions into users' native languages.

Currently the Consortium is running the largest anti-censorship operation serving 95% of the circumvention traffic from about 2 million users.

Our services are not limited to Chinese users. Within two days in January, 2008, we witnessed on our system users from 33 out of the 43 countries identified as "Not Free" by Freedom House's Freedom of the Press 2008 Survey, GPass has become a favorite with Iranians ever since it released a Farsi (Persian) version.

Our services have also benefited US-based organizations such as HRIC, the Chinese Democracy Party, VOA, and RFA.

Our Challenges

As a grassroots organization, we feel we have been fighting against a Goliath in cyberspace alone. Challenges we have been facing include:

1. Censors using high-tech equipment with ever-increasing performance for Internet snooping and control. The intelligence of our adversary, as well as our own system, learns and evolves with time and with experience, and with high-end machinery.
   Although we have not physically seen the machines in the server room of those in charge of maintaining the Chinese Firewall, the advanced capabilities indicate they constantly upgrade their hardware with top-of-the-line items on the market.
2. Resource limitations. So far our endeavor has been sustained mostly by volunteers. On the one hand, more and more users are eager to get on our Underground Railroad; on the other hand, we have limited bandwidth, hardware, manpower, and time to expand and satisfy their needs.
   I believe we have the most advanced anti-censorship technologies around. That is why we are ahead of the game most of the time, and why we have been able to support an ever-increasing user base. But technology is not the only determining factor. The game is now boiling down to a battle of resources. Besides the hardware of the Great Firewall, the censors have also assembled an army of tens of

thousands of net police to serve as a human flesh Great Firewall. That is a challenge for us because our current resources make it difficult if not near-impossible to match that kind of manpower. On the other hand, our experience indicates every penny we invest in our offense will force the censors to burn a dollar or more in defense. So every penny counts a lot in our effort.

3. Attacks from all directions. The Chinese Communist Party (CCP) has no interest in playing a fair cat-and-mouse game on the Internet. It constantly launches cyber attacks on our infrastructure and our people. Attempts to hack our websites are non-stop, emails impersonating our own people with virus attachments are abundant, harassing phone calls are not rare events. It even resorted to physical violence on U.S. soil when other measures failed: Armed Asian men broke into the home of the president of our organization, Yuan Li, in Atlanta, brutally beat him and stole his computers while leaving other valuables intact. We have reason to believe the CCP was behind the attacks.

As a side note, we would also like to point out that it seems the CCP has been using our systems as practice targets before it launches attacks against US and other countries' government networks. The tactics used in these attacks share much similarity with what we have seen.

Besides the direct attacks, the Chinese regime has also forced anti-virus companies in China to identify our software tools as viruses to discourage users from adopting the software. Surprisingly, anti-virus companies in the US such as Symantec and Norton do not seem to want to be left behind as their anti-virus software also indiscriminately labels some of our tools as viruses. Our written clarification with them has fallen on deaf ears.

Despite all the difficulties, we have not wavered from our mission. Many of us have witnessed first-hand the Communists' brainwashing, hatred induction, and indoctrination, and we treasure the information freedom outside the Great Firewall. However, the people still confined within the Great Firewall need much more help. We urge government agencies, NGOs, and corporations to step in and contribute to these efforts.

For democratic governments, many actions can be taken to bring the anti-censorship endeavor to the next level. For example:

Provide resources to these efforts. This is the most effective support. Since anti-censorship technologies have matured and have been field-tested, most resources are now devoted to the operation of these systems instead of to research and development. The impact of such support would be immediately visible. The government should measure its achievements by not only the number of political prisoners released, but also the number of users who are enabled and empowered to access information freely.

Limit technology exports to repressive regimes. Evidence shows that the advanced Internet filtering technologies used in the Chinese Great Firewall are provided by Western companies. Democratic nations should impose restrictions on such exports as they can be exploited for future enhancements of the Firewall.

Establish a funding vehicle to rally financial and resource support from other organizations and corporations. In particular, those multi-national technology companies such as Yahoo! and Google that have said it is not "convenient" for them to provide an uncensored web to users in China could contribute to our efforts and we would be happy to step in.

The United States funded the creation of Internet a few decades ago. Now the Internet is used in repressive regimes as a powerful tool to suppress freedom and is being morphed into a dark weapon for cyber war targeting the US and other free nations. Please allow us to submit our humble opinion that defending the transparency and freedom of the Internet is of critical national interest and we believe the US government has a responsibility to play a much more active role in this endeavor.

The Roles of US Companies in China's Internet Censorship

There is unfortunately strong indication that companies in free societies such as Cisco may have involved in assisting the Chinese security services to monitor and censor the Internet, and persecute and prosecute Chinese citizens who just want to use Internet to access uncensored information and/or express their own views freely and peacefully.

In a 2002 Cisco (China) PowerPoint presentation entitled "An Overview on [China's] Public Security Industry," now in our possession, a Cisco (China) official in the Government Business Department listed the "Golden Shield Project" – the host project of China's Great Firewall – as one of Cisco's major target customers. One of the main objectives in that Project, defined in the Cisco document as the "Monitoring and Control System for Public Internet Information Security," was to "combat the 'Falun Gong' evil cult."

We must take note that the two words of evil cult, the rhetoric of the Chinese Communist Party to persecute Falun Gong, are not even quotation-marked in the presentation. The view taken of my fellow-practitioners in the PowerPoint document raises obvious and profound concerns about Cisco's culpability in an Internet monitoring and censorship regime that has diminished freedom, added to the power of a powerful dictatorship and, in pursuit of those goals, caused the arrest and frequent murder of innocents at the hands of China's Firewall bureaucracy.

In the following PowerPoint page headed "Cisco Opportunity [on the Golden Shield Project]," Cisco listed the following four areas of potential assistance to China/business opportunities:

- High start-point planning;
- High standard construction;
- Technical training; and
- Security and operation maintenance."

The above areas of potential assistance appear to flatly rebut Cisco's repeated and self-serving claims that it has merely sold routers and other equipment to China's security services and has not in any way assisted or participated in the Internet censorship and monitoring activities of those security services.

In the battle between our Consortium and the totalitarian Chinese authorities, it appears that Cisco is selling router equipment to the Chinese police authorities by offering censorship training and other supports. Our research shows that the main Internet censorship of China involves IP blocking, content filtering and connection reset, and DNS hijacking, and they are all done at the national gateway level. The infrastructure of China's Great Firewall shown by our research coincides with the layouts in Cisco (China)'s PowerPoint document.

We must appeal to these US corporations to reconsider what they are doing. Every time our anti-censorship tools are attacked using their technology, they are taking the side of the totalitarian authorities against Chinese people seeking some of the most basic of human rights. They are jeopardizing U.S. national security interests by directly compromising the safety of millions of Internet users in closed societies around the world. This is no longer just a virtual game, and it is certainly no longer just about dollars and cents. Real lives are at stake. Just ask Yahoo! how Mr. Shi Tao is faring as a prisoner of conscience facing several more years in his prison sentence for sending an email.

Our Consortium has been able to stay ahead of the censorship game by developing new software and new technology, but each battle has been grueling and certainly taps into our already scarce resources. Sometimes we feel like a little David fighting a constant battle with a monolithic Goliath out in cyberspace. It has been a lonely battle thus far and we are tired of having to fight our fellow American companies.

We intend to further investigate the history, use and meaning of the PowerPoint document, and to investigate all forms of assistance that Cisco officials may have given to China's Firewall and police bureaucracies in the latter's determined efforts suppress free Internet use and to brutally punish users and facilitators of uncensored Internet access. We call on Cisco to determine, on the basis of a thorough and searching investigation, the manner and extent to which the PowerPoint document was used and circulated within Cisco (China) and the extent to which the document's views were shared within Cisco (China). (We would like to know what the reaction of Cisco (China) officials was to the document's characterization of Falun Gong as evil.) We call on Cisco officials to acknowledge, immediately, once and for all and, at a minimum, that they can no longer assure Congress that Cisco (China) is and has been a merely passive seller of routers and other equipment to China's security services, and we further call on senior Cisco management to acknowledge that they can no longer assure Congress that Cisco (China) has not been and is not now an accomplice and partner in China's Internet repression and, whether directly or indirectly, its infamous "610 Office" persecution of Falun Gong practitioners in China.

A cloud of suspicion now hangs over Cisco, which self-serving assertions of innocence can no longer dispel. Nothing but the most thorough and independent investigation, which we hope will be closely monitored by this Committee, will remove the concern that, in its efforts to sell routers and other equipment to China's security police, Cisco (China) officials were complicit in the persecution of those who bravely work to end China's efforts to monopolize the free flow of information to, from and between its people.

We conclude by noting another form of censorship, namely, self-censorship by content providers or websites operators. International companies doing business in censorship countries, such as China, restrict themselves and provide tailored content to users in these regimes. A prime example is Google's Chinese version, which provides drastically different search results for queries originating in China from its versions in other locations. As a U.S.

company that appears not to be aligned with the repressive forces in China, Google's collusion and collaboration with the repressive weapons of censorship make the efforts of those seeking to expose the Chinese people to the market place of ideas all the more difficult. Unfortunately, there exist no effective technical measures to overcome this form of censorship.

So far the public have learned about Google's self-censorship mainly through media reports and rights organizations. Google itself has been silent about it. We believe that all Google users and shareholders deserve to know exactly what Google does to the 230 million Chinese Internet users. We therefore created the "Google Search Review" service, http://gg.edoors.com, that compares search results from google.com and google.cn.

We would like to offer the code to this Committee and to Google, and we respectfully request Google to host this service on their servers, and announce it to the public.

In: Promoting Global Internet Freedom
Editor: Samantha R. Weber
ISBN: 978-1-61728-827-2

Chapter 9

TESTIMONY OF ALAN DAVIDSON, DIRECTOR OF PUBLIC POLICY, GOOGLE INC., BEFORE THE CONGRESSIONAL-EXECUTIVE COMMISSION ON CHINA, HEARING ON "GOOGLE AND INTERNET CONTROL IN CHINA: A NEXUS BETWEEN HUMAN RIGHTS AND TRADE?"

Alan Davidson

Chairman Dorgan, Chairman Levin, and Members of the Commission.

Thank you for bringing attention to the important issue of Internet censorship, and for giving Google the opportunity to discuss today·s global challenges to freedom of expression and access to information online. Internet censorship is a growing global problem. It not only raises important human rights concerns, but also creates significant barriers for U.S. companies doing business abroad. As Google's Director of Public Policy in the Americas, I am part of the Google team that works to promote free speech both in the U.S. and globally.

The number of governments that routinely censor the Internet has grown from a handful in 2002 to more than 40 countries today. Even in countries that are just beginning to make the Internet available to their citizens, governments are simultaneously building sophisticated tools for blocking and censoring content. Repressive regimes are developing ever more advanced tools to use against dissidents and are sharing censorship tactics across borders. Human rights observers have noted that these governments are baking in censorship tools for the Internet rather than chasing after criticism that has already been aired.

The lack of transparency and accountability in blocking and censoring is also a grave concern. Over the last several years, we have seen an increasing number of governments, even democratic ones, choose to blacklist certain sites they deem harmful without providing any formal oversight of process or meaningful ability to appeal. In the next few years, the Open Net Initiative predicts that we will see more targeted surveillance and increasingly sophisticated malware being used to make the monitoring and documentation of government activity even harder.

But despite these challenges we remain optimistic about the ability of technology to empower individuals and realize the potential for a global Internet community. We believe that maximizing the free flow of information online can help to increase openness and prosperity even in closed societies.

As Google invests in new countries, we look to the following three principles to help us protect online freedom of speech and increase access to information:

- **Access** - maximizing access to information on the Web and tools for the creation of content.
- **Transparency** - notifying users when information has been removed by government demand.
- **Trust** - retaining the trust of our users by protecting their privacy and security from governmental acts intended to chill speech.

With those principles in mind, we would like to address four main issues in this testimony:

First, Googles situation in China.

Second, the global challenges Google and other U.S. companies face every day from governments who seek to limit free expression online.

Third, the economic implications of censorship.

And finally, the need for governments around the world to do more to reduce Internet censorship and support free expression online.

CHINA UPDATE

Let us start with an update on Googles situation in China.

We launched Google.cn, our Chinese search engine, in January 2006 in the belief that the benefits of increased access to information for people in China and a more open Internet outweighed our discomfort in agreeing to censor some results. While we have faced challenges, especially in the last 12 to 18 months, we have also had some success.

Google has become the second most popular search engine in China, behind Baidu, and we were the first search engine in China to let users know when results had been removed to comply with Chinese law. Use of our maps, mobile and translation services has grown quickly. And from a business perspective, while our China revenues are still small in the context of our larger business, the last quarter of 2009 was our most successful quarter ever in China.

However, in the last year we have seen increasing attempts to limit free speech on the Web in China. Numerous sites including YouTube, The Guardian, Facebook, Twitter, Blogger and Wikipedia have been blocked, some of them indefinitely. In addition, last June the Chinese government announced that all personal computers sold in China would need to be pre-loaded with software that could be used to censor online content. After a public outcry and pressure from companies, the proposal was later withdrawn.

Most recently, in mid-December, we detected a highly sophisticated and targeted attack on our corporate infrastructure originating from China. What at first appeared to be an isolated security incident - albeit a significant one - turned out upon investigation to be something quite different.

First of all, at least twenty other large companies from a wide range of businesses - including the Internet, finance, technology, media and chemical sectors - were similarly targeted.

Second, we believe that a primary, albeit unsuccessful, goal of the attack was to access Gmail accounts surreptitiously.

Third, we discovered in our investigation that the accounts of dozens of U.S.-, China- and European-based Gmail users who are advocates of human rights in China appear to have been routinely accessed by third parties. I want to make clear that this happened independent of the security breach to Google, most likely via phishing scams or malware placed on the users computers.

The attack on our corporate infrastructure and the surveillance it uncovered - as well as attempts over the past year to limit free speech on the

Web even further – led us to conclude that we were no longer willing to censor our search results in China. This decision was in keeping with our pledge when we launched Google.cn that we would carefully monitor conditions in China, including new laws and other restrictions on our services.

I want to stress that while we know these attacks came from China, we are not prepared to say who carried out these attacks. We do know such attacks are violations of Chinas own laws and we would hope that the Chinese authorities will work with US officials to investigate this matter.

Earlier this week we stopped censoring our search services – Google Search, Google News, and Google Images – on Google.cn. Users visiting Google.cn are now being redirected to Google.com.hk, where we are offering uncensored search in simplified Chinese, specifically designed for users in mainland China and delivered via our servers in Hong Kong.

Figuring out how to make good on our promise to stop censoring search on Google.cn has been hard. We want as many people in the world as possible to have access to our services, including users in mainland China, yet the Chinese government has been crystal clear throughout our discussions that self-censorship is a non-negotiable legal requirement. We believe this new approach of providing uncensored search in simplified Chinese from Google.com.hk is a practical solution to the challenges weve faced - its entirely legal and will meaningfully increase access to information for people in China. We are well aware that the Chinese government can, at any time, block access to our services - indeed we have already seen intermittent censorship of certain search queries on both Google.com.hk and Google.com.

In terms of Googles wider business operations, we intend to continue R&D work in China and also to maintain a sales presence there, though the size of the sales team will obviously be partially dependent on the ability of mainland Chinese users to access Google.com.hk.

Before moving on to the broader, global challenges Google faces, we would like to make clear that all these decisions have been driven and implemented by our executives in the United States, and that none of our employees in China can, or should, be held responsible for them. Despite all the uncertainty and difficulties they have faced since we made our announcement in January, they have continued to focus on serving our Chinese users and customers. We are immensely proud of them.

OTHER GLOBAL CHALLENGES AND ECONOMIC IMPLICATIONS

China is simply one example of a global phenomenon that raises concerns. Google has become a regular focus of governmental efforts to limit individual expression because our technologies and services enable people with Internet connections to speak to a worldwide audience.

More than 25 governments have blocked Google services over the past few years. Since 2007, YouTube has been blocked in over a dozen countries. We have received reports that our blogging platform has been blocked in at least seven countries, and that our social networking site, Orkut, has been blocked in several countries.

Iran provides a prominent recent example of political censorship. This past June, during the protests that followed the presidential election in Iran, the government of Iran ejected foreign journalists, shut down the national media and disrupted Internet and cell phone service. In spite of this, YouTube and Twitter were cited by traditional journalists and bloggers alike as the best source for firsthand accounts and on-the-scene footage of the protests and violence in Tehran.

The Iran example demonstrates why its imperative for governments, companies, and individuals to do more to ensure that the Internet continues to be a powerful medium for expressing political opinions, religious views and other core speech without restriction.

But the debate on Internet censorship is, of course, not only about human rights. At issue is the continued economic growth spurred by a free and globally accessible Internet. Barriers to the free flow of information online have significant and serious economic implications: they impose often one-sided restrictions on the services of U.S. and global Internet companies, while also impeding other businesses who depend on the Internet to reach their customers.

When a foreign government pursues censorship policies in a manner that favors domestic Internet companies, this goes against basic international trade principles of non-discrimination and maintaining a level playing field. Local competitors gain a business advantage, and consumers are deprived of the ability to choose the best services for their needs. And when a government disrupts an Internet service in its entirety – *e.g.*, blocking an entire website because of concerns with a handful of user-generated postings – the government is restricting trade well-beyond what would be required even if it had a legitimate public policy justification for the censorship.

Opaque censorship restrictions can also be very damaging to the host nation, because they undermine the rule of law and make it very hard for foreign companies to navigate within the law, which has negative consequences in terms of foreign direct investment.

The U.S. government has taken some positive steps to address the means and effects of censorship through trade tools. The United States Trade Representative has sought explicitly to address some of these issues in trade agreements –most recently, in the U.S.-Korea Free Trade Agreement - and we applaud these efforts. And the Commerce Department and USTR have been helpful in the context of particular incidents we have encountered in the past.

But governments need to develop a full set of new trade rules to address new trade barriers. We encourage further efforts along these lines, by the U.S. government and other governments to redress favoritism shown by some governments for indigenous companies over U.S.-based corporations. We should continue to look for effective ways to address unfair foreign trade barriers in the online world: to use trade agreements, trade tools, and trade diplomacy to promote the free flow of information on the Internet.

How Governments Can Support Free Expression

Internet censorship is a challenge that no particular industry - much less any single company - can tackle on its own. However, we believe concerted, collective action by governments, companies and individuals can help promote online free expression and reduce the impact of censorship.

As I noted previously, our business is based on the three principles of access, transparency, and retaining the trust of online users. These principles are not exclusive to Google, and there are ways that the public and private sectors can work together to advance them.

First, making every effort at both the grassroots and government level to maximize access to information online. The State Department recently issued a request for proposals on projects to help citizens on the ground access information they would not otherwise be able to share or receive. Google supports the joint commitment of Congress and the Obama Administration to provide funds to groups around the world to make sure people who need to access the Internet safely get the right training and tools. This is a great step forward, and we believe much more can be done to support grassroots organizations that develop technology to combat Internet censorship.

Second, establishing transparency as a norm when governments attempt to censor or request information about users, or even when a company's network comes under attack. This is a critical part of the democratic process, and governments must strike a balance between law enforcement and proper disclosure, allowing citizens to hold their lawmakers accountable. In many cases the cloud of secrecy around cyber attacks only works to the attackers' advantage because it enables them to operate more easily under the radar. Some of the sensible ideas we've heard discussed to improve transparency include: requiring annual company reports on the levels of filtering being complied with and requests for personally identifiable information from government officials; and greater engagement by the U.S. government with countries that censor the Internet, so any company disclosures result in concrete actions by the U.S. government.

Third, retaining users' trust by committing to protect their privacy and security. There is nothing new about governments using surveillance and intimidation tactics to chill speech about uncomfortable ideas. What is new is the growing deployment of online surveillance toward these ends. To be clear, we fully support lawful investigation by government authorities to protect individuals and companies. But we are committed to protecting our users against unlawful and overbroad government demands for their personal information and ensuring the security of our networks. The global trend toward increasing government access to online communications is of great concern and demands serious review and oversight. In addition, the U.S. should push for improved international cooperation to protect user privacy.

We are also grateful for the efforts of lawmakers to bring more companies into the Global Network Initiative (GNI). As a platform for companies, human rights groups, investors, and academics, the GNI requires its members to commit to standards that respect and protect user rights to privacy and freedom of expression. Additional corporate participation will help the GNI reach its full potential – and we look to the Members of this Commission for continued leadership.

And finally, ensuring that the U.S. government makes the issue of Internet openness, including the free flow of information, an important part of foreign policy, trade, development and human rights engagement. This includes prioritizing the issue as a matter of U.S. foreign policy, including in various dialogues that the U.S. government pursues with regimes that are heavy Internet restrictors; using trade tools where possible; and perhaps also making it part of the criteria for receiving development aid. Ultimately, governments that respect the right to online free expression should work together to craft new international rules to better discipline government actions that impede the free flow of information over the Internet. We need forward-looking rules that provide maximum protection against the trade barriers of the new technology era.

On the multilateral human rights front, enforcing and supporting the mechanisms of the International Covenant on Civil and Political Rights and others under the UN system (*e.g.*, the UN Human Rights Committee) to demand accountability from governments for Internet censorship is helpful. At the very least, these mechanisms can be better used to shine light on government abuses.

CONCLUSION

We would like to thank Chairman Dorgan, Chairman Levin, the members of the Congressional-Executive Commission on China, and other Members of Congress who have spoken in support of upholding the right to online free expression around the world. It is only with the attention and involvement of leaders like yourselves that we can make real progress in the effort to protect these basic human rights. We look forward to working with you and other government officials to find viable solutions to maximize access to information, increase transparency and protect users around the world.

In: Promoting Global Internet Freedom
Editor: Samantha R. Weber
ISBN: 978-1-61728-827-2

Chapter 10

Statement of Christine N. Jones, Executive Vice-President, General Counsel, & Corporate Secretary, The Go Daddy Group, Inc., before the Congressional-Executive Commission on China, Hearing on "Google and Internet Control in China: A Nexus between Human Rights and Trade?"

Christine N. Jones

Introduction

Thank you, Chairman Dorgan, and members of the Commission, for the honor of testifying here today. We at Go Daddy applaud the actions of the Commission to support the continuing global exchange of information and trade on the Internet.

BACKGROUND

The recent cyber attacks on Google and other U.S. companies are troubling, but they reflect a situation that The Go Daddy Group has been combating for many years. Go Daddy is an Arizona company which consists of eight ICANN-accredited registrars, including GoDaddy.com, Inc., the world's largest domain name registrar. This month, Go Daddy passed a major Internet milestone – we now have more than 40 million domain names under management, more than any other company in the history of the Internet. We are also the largest provider of shared website hosting. We have more than 7 million paying customers located all over the globe. So, if you are an active Internet user with a domain name or a website, the likelihood is that at some point you have utilized Go Daddy's services to engage on the Internet.

Go Daddy's customer base includes tens of thousands of Chinese nationals. We work with Chinese customers on a daily basis to help them to establish an identity on the Internet, and to ensure the secure and seamless operation of their hosted websites. We are also constantly in the process of repelling cyber attacks against the systems and infrastructure that secure our customers' websites and Internet activities. A large percentage of those attacks can be traced to China, as can other illegal activities that interfere with our customers' safe and productive use of the Internet. I am here today to share some of our experiences as they relate to China, specifically with respect to the following: increased monitoring and surveillance of .CN domain name registrations; increasing DDoS attacks originating in China; spam; payment fraud; and, what we would like to see the US Government do to help alleviate some of these issues.

INCREASED MONITORING AND SURVEILLANCE OF .CN REGISTRATIONS

There appears to be a recent increase in China's surveillance and monitoring of the Internet activities of its citizens. As a domain name registrar, Go Daddy provides registration services for numerous top level domain names. Top level domains, or "TLDs," are the suffix that appears at the end of a domain name (for example, .COM, .NET, etc.). One of the TLDs we have historically offered is .CN, the Chinese country code top level domain (or "ccTLD"). Go Daddy is authorized by the China Internet Network Information

Centre (known as the CNNIC), a quasi-governmental agency in China, to offer registration services for the .CN ccTLD. Go Daddy began to offer the .CN ccTLD in April of 2005 and, at this time we have approximately 27,000 .CN domain names under management. Registering a domain name with the .CN ccTLD is an important step for any individual or company wishing to establish an audience or business foothold in the Chinese market.

When Go Daddy started registering the .CN TLD in 2005, CNNIC required us to collect the contact information of the individual or company registering the domain name. The required contact information included first and last names of the registrant, his or her physical address, telephone number and email address. The extent of the personal information collected was typical of what is normally required by .ccTLD registries.

A little over four months ago, on December 12, 2009, CNNIC announced that it was implementing a new policy relating to the registration of .CN domain names, and that it would begin to enforce the new policy effective December 14, 2009. The policy required that any registrants of new .CN domain names provide color headshot photo identification, business identification (including a Chinese business registration number), and physical signed registration forms. This information was to be collected by the registrar, and then forwarded to CNNIC for its review prior to the activation of the registration.

Less than a month later, on January 5, 2010, CNNIC announced that Chinese nationals were no longer permitted to register domain names through non-Chinese registrars. In accordance with the new policy, Go Daddy halted all new .CN registrations.

On February 3, 2010, CNNIC announced that it would reopen .CN domain name registrations to overseas registrars. However, the stringent new identification and documentation procedures would remain in effect. CNNIC also announced an audit of all .CN domain name registrations *currently* held by Chinese nationals. Domain name registrars, including Go Daddy, were then instructed to obtain photo identification, business identification, and physical signed registration forms from all *existing* .CN domain name registrants who are Chinese nationals, and to provide copies of those documents to CNNIC. We were advised that domain names of registrants who did not register as required would no longer resolve. In other words, their domain names would no longer work.

We were immediately concerned about the motives behind the increased level of registrant verification being required by CNNIC. It did not make sense to us that the identification procedures that had been in place since 2005 were apparently no longer sufficient from China's standpoint, and no convincing rationale for the increase in documentation was offered. We were also concerned by the *ex post facto* nature of the new requirement – in other words, at the time the affected Chinese nationals registered their domain names, they were not required to provide photo identification and the other documentation now being required by the CNNIC. The new documentation requirement was to be retroactively applied to registrants who had previously registered their websites, in some cases years before. The intent of the new procedures appeared, to us, to be based on a desire by the Chinese authorities to exercise increased control over the subject matter of domain name registrations by Chinese nationals.

Approximately 1,200 unique Go Daddy customers were affected by CNNIC's *ex post facto* application of the requirement for additional identification documentation. This represented a much larger number of domain names, of course, because many registrants have multiple domain names under their control. We contacted our affected customers advising of this new requirement, and advised them that, if they wished to provide us with the required documentation, we would provide it to CNNIC in accordance with CNNIC's directive. Ultimately, only about 20% of the affected customers submitted the required documentation and agreed to allow us to submit it to the CNNIC. The domain names of the remaining 900 or so customers remain at risk of cancellation. That means thousands of websites the Chinese authorities may successfully disable because of retroactive application of this new set of rules.

Go Daddy has been registering domain names since 2000. We currently serve as an authorized registrar for dozens of domain name extensions. This is the first time a registry has asked us to retroactively obtain additional verification and documentation of individuals who have registered a domain name through our company. We are concerned for the security of the individuals affected by CNNIC's new requirements, as well as for the chilling effect we believe the requirements will have on new .CN domain name registrations. For these reasons, we have decided to discontinue offering new .CN domain names at this time. We continue to manage the .CN domain names of our existing customers.

INCREASING DDOS ATTACKS ORIGINATING IN CHINA

Another China-related issue we have seen recently is an increase in the number of distributed denial of service (also known as "DDoS") attacks on the systems that host our customer websites. In Go Daddy's case, a DDoS attack is typically an attempt to make websites that we host unavailable to their intended users for some period of time. We also combat many attacks that are more systematic, such as hackers attempting to insert malicious code into the pages of our customers' hosted websites. An example of this type of attack would be the installation of spyware on the computers of all visitors to a website we host. The spyware then logs keystrokes to harvest passwords to email accounts, which can then be infiltrated and monitored without the knowledge of the account owner.

Go Daddy operates data centers, and has invested hundreds of millions of dollars in those centers, including building and operating state-of-the-art security measures that monitor and fight external attacks on our systems 24 hours a day, 365 days a year. In the first three months of this year, we have repelled dozens of extremely serious DDoS attacks that appear to have originated in China, based on the IP addresses from which the attacks derived. Had our security systems not countered these attacks, the result would have been a widespread take-down of our customers' hosted websites.

Spam

Unlike many other Internet companies of our size, Go Daddy operates a large 24/7 Abuse Department whose mission it is to identify and help stop illegal and malicious activity on the Internet. We work very closely with local, federal and international law enforcement agencies to stop all types of Internet abuse, including child pornographers, unauthorized online pharmacies, spammers, phishers, and sellers of counterfeit merchandise.

In monitoring spam activities, we have found that an overwhelming majority of websites promoted through spam are hosted in China, often at service providers that choose to ignore complaints of spam and other types of illegal activity. When Go Daddy and other legitimate hosting companies receive complaints that spam is being sent from websites hosted by their company, the sites are typically taken offline. However, many companies in China offer so-called bulletproof hosting, where websites are allowed to stay online and spam operations can continue unabated, even after receipt of a complaint.

China is also the location of choice for buying and selling lists of spam "zombies" - personal computers deliberately infected with spam-enabling viruses and operated by ordinary, usually oblivious, computer users around the world. Our research indicates that China dominates the market for buying and selling lists of zombie PCs, which are peddled by virus writers on Internet forums found on Chinese servers. Lists can currently be had for about $2,000-$3,000 per 20,000 compromised computers.

Another reason so much spam appears to originate in China is the spam industry's growing sophistication. The modern spam industry is populated by technically advanced programmers and organized crime rings. Spammers create complex phishing scams to lure individuals to fake websites where they are conned into divulging bank account, social security and credit card details. Organized spam groups tend to avoid operating in jurisdictions where authorities are hostile and penalties potentially severe. To date, China has not enforced significant penalties against spammers and others who utilize the Internet to engage in criminal activities; thus, it has become a sort of safe harbor for such criminals.

China is also an attractive locale from which spammers operate because of its low costs. A domain name can be bought for as little as $0.15 in China, which allows scammers to acquire lots of domain names inexpensively. Domain names cost much more in the United States, where some of the money goes to fighting abuse and spam. But the low revenue stream in China is likely hampering the creation of programs to stop abuse.

China today is basically the only major market where spammers can do just about anything they want. Go Daddy's efforts to persuade authorities there to investigate or prosecute spammers have been ineffective, as have our efforts to work with Chinese- based hosting companies to shut down compromised websites. Official pronouncements by the Chinese government usually appear to be aimed at getting Chinese spam servers removed from foreign blacklists rather than actually preventing spam.

PAYMENT FRAUD

In addition to our Abuse department, Go Daddy also has a full time Fraud department that is continually monitoring and guarding against payment fraud issues affecting our customers. The payment fraud trends associated with China-based users include the widespread use of compromised U.S. or UK credit cards to purchase items. In one particularly egregious case, an individual or group operating from China is utilizing compromised credit cards from a wide variety of banks to purchase one year domain name registrations. The registrant then attempts to use the domain names to perform a variety of illegal activities. Since January, our Fraud team has managed to close 134 new shopper accounts associated with this repeat Chinese fraudster.

Go Daddy has also been successful in combating Chinese spammers by closing customer accounts through our payment fraud process. Most recently, our Abuse department identified a Chinese-based spammer with 175 separate shopper accounts with Go Daddy. Although each of the accounts was opened using a valid PayPal account, we were able to halt the spammer's activities by placing a payment fraud lock on the accounts.

In addition to the challenges presented by China-based criminals, societal and cultural norms in China can make it difficult to identify and resolve payment fraud issues affecting legitimate Chinese customers. For instance, a problem we frequently encounter is the provision of invalid shopper/billing information by Chinese shoppers. Where invalid information is provided, contacting the customer to verify order activity is usually impossible.

Credit card use is not prevalent in China, and most Chinese shoppers do not possess their own credit card. When credit cards are issued, they are often shared by numerous individuals. It is therefore very common for accounts owned by Chinese shoppers to have multiple unrelated names and addresses on file. This too makes identifying payment fraud more difficult.

Despite these payment fraud challenges, Go Daddy is focused on continuing to serve and expand upon its Chinese customer base. In furtherance of this goal, in December 2009, we began to offer the Alipay payment processing system to our customers. Alipay is China's leading independent third-party online payment platform, with more than 270 million registered users. What sets Alipay apart from other online payment platforms is that it holds funds in escrow until the product is received. Chinese customers can fund their Alipay accounts using direct bank payments or debit cards, both of which are more common forms of payment in China than credit cards. Alipay is a popular and trusted option for Chinese consumers, and we have experienced a large increase in our volume of sales to Chinese customers since we implemented it as a payment option. We have also found use of the Alipay system to be very helpful in combating China-related payment fraud. In fact, our new shopper payment fraud rates associated with Chinese accounts has been reduced by approximately 50% since we introduced Alipay in December of 2009.

What the U.S. Government can do to Help

Go Daddy's primary mission is to promote secure, easy, equal access to the Internet to people around the world. We are also committed to ending illegal or nefarious uses of the Internet, including for the invasion of personal privacy or to limit freedom of expression. We believe that many of the current abuses of the Internet originating in China are due to a lack of enforcement against criminal activities by the Chinese government. Our experience has been that China is focused on using the Internet to monitor and control the legitimate activities of its citizens, rather than penalizing those who commit Internet-related crimes.

We believe that countries or individuals that engage in cyber attacks or other types of Internet crimes should face serious consequences and international condemnation. We hope that the U.S. government can use its influence with authorities in China to increase Chinese enforcement activities relating to Internet abuse, while encouraging the free exchange of ideas, information, and trade. This would include the retraction of China's recent policies relating to the registration of .CN domain names, which will act as a barrier to Internet access by Chinese nationals.

In: Promoting Global Internet Freedom
Editor: Samantha R. Weber
ISBN: 978-1-61728-827-2

Chapter 11

TESTIMONY OF SHARON HOM, EXECUTIVE DIRECTOR, HUMAN RIGHTS IN CHINA, BEFORE THE CONGRESSIONAL-EXECUTIVE COMMISSION ON CHINA, HEARING ON "GOOGLE AND INTERNET CONTROL IN CHINA: A NEXUS BETWEEN HUMAN RIGHTS AND TRADE?"

Sharon Hom

Mr. Chairman, thank you for inviting Human Rights in China (HRIC) to testify at this important and timely hearing. As a Chinese human rights NGO, HRIC appreciates this opportunity to share our experience and some modest recommendations. In light of the events of the past week, the topic for today is a story still in progress.

The loss of annual MFN review leverage in 2000 and a decade of delinking of human rights from trade has contributed to the lack of systematic and sustainable human rights progress, and an unstable, unpredictable climate for foreign business in China. In recent months, there have also been disturbing reports about a series of cyber-attacks, including the one publicized by Google in January of this year, emanating from China, targeting foreign governments, private businesses, and human rights advocates both in the United States and around the world. These cyber-attacks present serious cross-border human rights, diplomatic, and business challenges for China and the world.[1]

As the comprehensive CECC Annual Report for 2009, the State Department Country report for China, and recent United Nations human rights reviews of China's record demonstrate, human rights violations in China – a country vital to U.S. security, trade, and human rights policy interests – remain serious, systematic, and widespread.[2] On top of the economic, political, and increasing soft power leverage of China, China exerts control over expression on the Internet through its state-of-the arts technology, state secrets and state security system, police and security apparatus, and resulting self-censorship.[3] By doing so, the Chinese government's policy and practices on information control implicate two universally recognized and mutually reinforcing human rights – the right to freedom of expression and opinion and the right to privacy.[4]

The experiences of HRIC's own staff also illustrate that the Chinese authorities' repressive tactics at home extend to Chinese nationals and human rights defenders abroad. Such tactics include blacklisting, surveillance, and even inhumane denials of permission to return to China for family funerals. Additionally, the Chinese authorities have succeeded in preventing independent human rights NGO dedicated to China from succeeding in applying for ECO SOC status or UN conferences' accreditation – thereby undermining independent Chinese NGO voices.

Role of Technology

The rapid pace of technology developments globally and in China, including in mobile and connective technologies, has provided tools for increased social control and human rights violations in China, especially regarding freedom of expression and privacy. However, China's Great Fire Wall is impressive, but clearly not impregnable, as technology developments also provide tools for advancing fundamental rights and democracy in China. With over 384 million citizens online, 600 million mobile phone users, and between 26,000 to 30,000 Tweeters, all despite China's censorship regime, China is a prime target country for developing empowering potential uses for new technology, which will also have significant implications for the region and for the future security and viability of the Internet worldwide.

For more than two decades now, HRIC has focused on supporting Chinese lawyers, activists, journalists, writers, and other rights defenders in China. From our China office in Hong Kong, and our U.S. office in New York, and with a committed staff with Chinese and international law, technology, and media expertise, we have also been developing and deploying a range of technology approaches and tools to promote uncensored information flow into and out of China. Using Internet technology that bypasses China's censorship mechanism, HRIC has provided and continues to provide an uncensored platform for Chinese voices and disseminates independent news, discussion, and rights-related electronic publications through stable mass e-mail delivery to over 200,000 subscribers in every province and autonomous region in China.

HRIC's electronic publications provide access to proxy servers and six interrelated websites offering online Chinese publications, tools for activists, and online advocacy resources. Analysis of e-mail delivery rates indicate that since a new electronic biweekly was launched in June 2009, an average of 74% of biweekly e-newsletters reached the first Simple Mail Transfer Protocol (SMTP) server in mainland China. This program has enabled individuals in China, through the use of proxy technology and other circumvention tools, to have uncensored access to human rights information on the Internet and a space for debate and discussion. HRIC incorporated YouTube and Twitter into its advocacy strategy last year as well, launching an HRIC YouTube channel and regularly tweeting the latest human rights developments.

THE CASE OF LIU XIAOBO: WHO'S AFRAID OF THE INTERNET?

There is perhaps no better example of the Chinese government's anxiety underlying the official crackdown on freedom of expression on the Internet than the case of Liu Xiaobo, a prominent independent intellectual in China, long-time advocate of political reform and human rights in China, and outspoken critic of the Chinese communist regime.

On Christmas Day, 2009, a court in Beijing convicted Liu Xiaobo of "inciting subversion of state power" and sentenced him to 11 years in prison and two years of deprivation of political rights. The verdict cited as evidence passages from six essays Liu published online between 2005 and 2007 and his role in drafting *Charter 08*, an online petition for democratic reform issued on

December 9, 2008, which has since garnered more than 10,000 signatures, predominantly from Chinese in China. On February 9, 2010, a higher court rejected Liu's appeal and upheld the verdict.[5]

Liu Xiaobo's case elucidates one of the most crucial challenges facing the emerging Chinese civil society: the clash of visions between Chinese pressing for a democratic China governed by genuine rule of law, and the Chinese authorities, who demonstrate time and again their intolerance for diverse views and their need to maintain control at all cost. The outcome of Liu's case has made clear the authorities' willingness to trample on a fundamental human right protected in the Chinese Constitution and enshrined in international human rights law. It also raises serious concerns about the prospects for the rule of law, human rights, and democracy in China.

Liu's six essays cited in the verdict were the following:

- **The CPC's Dictatorial Patriotism** (posted on Epochtimes.com and 5 links): Liu debunks the notion successfully purveyed by the CPC that the ruling party is the Chinese nation itself, a fallacious concept that has enabled it to maintain absolute rule over the people.

- **The Many Aspects of CPC Dictatorship** (512 clicks; posted on observechina.net; secretchina.com): Liu describes the post-Mao regime—unlike that during the era of "Maoist totalitarianism"—as more skillful in using "pragmatic, flexible control methods" to maintain stability. Liu warns that "[t]he loyalty bought by the promise of a comfortable life has a soul that is rotten to the core," and that the system is ultimately unsustainable.

- **Can It be that the Chinese People Deserve Only "Party-Led Democracy"?** (402 clicks; posted on epochtimes.com; observechina.net): Liu points out that the Chinese people—having been conditioned historically to view any benevolent policy as mercy granted by their ruler—are in fact complicit in their own oppression. Rather than waiting for the arrival of a "virtuous master," they must, Liu maintains, place their hope in the "continuous expansion of the 'new power' among the people."

- **Changing the Regime by Changing Society** (748 clicks; posted on epochtimes.com; observechina.net): Liu explores how a continuously growing civil society is the key to China's gradual, bottom-up transformation into a free society.

- **The Negative Effects of the Rise of Dictatorship on World Democratization** (57 clicks; posted on observechina.net; secretchina.com): Liu discusses China's use of "money diplomacy" to degrade world civilization, and the necessity of helping the world's largest dictatorship transform into a free and democratic country with direct consequences for global democratization.

- **Further Questions About Child Slavery in China's Kilns** (488 clicks; posted on minzhuzhongguo.org; renyurenquan.org): Liu examines the extreme government corruption and lack of accountability that have enabled thousands of children to be kidnapped and used as slaves in kiln factories.

The verdict also cited ***Charter 08*** (**5154** clicks; posted on chinesepen.org, boxun.org, minzhuzhongguo.org).

Liu Xiaobo was a principal drafter of *Charter 08*, an appeal for fundamental political transformation and for the implementation of key foundational principles—freedom, human rights, and equality, among others. The document also lists 19 essential features of a new, democratic government, including legislative democracy, judicial independence, urban-rural equality, freedom of association, assembly, expression and religion, social security, and transitional justice.

In their argument at trial, Liu's defense lawyers pointed out that the articles and *Charter 08* were posted on websites based outside China, not accessible by people inside China. However, the court's verdict provided the total number of clicks, as of December 23, 2009, on the articles and *Charter 08* as 7,361 (with the clicks on specific items ranging from a low of 57 to a high of 5,154). Even if all the clicks were made by Chinese citizens inside China, and even if each click represents a different visitor, the total number of people is an infinitesimally small portion of China's population of 1.3 billion.

If 7,361 people reading these documents can, in the view of the Chinese authorities, pose such a grave threat, whatever that reveals about the sense of security among those in power, Liu Xiaobo's case is also a testament to the power and necessity of freedom of expression.

In addition to the high-profile case of Liu Xiaobo, there are countless other examples of China's use of the crime of "incitement to subvert state power" to punish expression on the Internet. Scholars, journalists, artists, lawyers, and rights activists have all found themselves prosecuted for "incitement to subvert state power," for doing nothing more than exercising their rights to freedom of expression and opinion online. As a consequence of using the Internet as a platform to speak out on such important issues as democratic reform, laborers' rights, state confiscation of lands, earthquake victims' rights, and government corruption, these individuals have been sentenced to draconian prison terms, some lasting more than a decade. In 2009, HRIC issued press releases on at least 12 individuals who had come under official scrutiny for their activities on the Internet.[6]

LOOKING AHEAD AND RECOMMENDATIONS

In the fall of 2012, the Communist Party of China (CPC) will hold the 18th National People's Congress. Due to term restrictions, Hu Jintao, the current President of the People's Republic of China, will be required to step down as the party's General Secretary at that time. The 18th National People's Congress will therefore be the first time in the CPC's history that a meeting to redistribute power will be held without a political strongman casting his shadow over it. It will decide on the dominant power in China's politics for the following five to ten years.[7]

The political contest surrounding the 18th National People's Congress is already having a clear effect on the current political situation in China. The pattern in the past has been that during the process of power transition within the CPC, various factions exhibit exceptional toughness in order to demonstrate their ideological orthodoxy and thus gain the upper hand in the power struggle. The comprehensive tightening of social controls by Chinese authorities since last year and their recent tough attitude in dealing with a series of both domestic and foreign events is a manifestation of this effect. One should not expect there to be any relaxation of this posture before the 18th National People's Congress convenes in 2012.

While the political climate for the next few years may not be encouraging, there are still concrete actions that the U.S. government and the private sector can take.

- **Individual cases:** In line with the U.S. government's renewed engagement with the UN Human Rights Council, the U.S. can **press for releases of individuals as part of China's compliance with decisions of independent UN human rights mechanisms such as the Working Group on Arbitrary Detention**, which has issued decisions on cases such as those of Shi Tao and Jin Haike.[8]

- **Promoting empowering uses of technology:** The past decades of rapid-paced technology developments in China demonstrate that there is no one silver bullet for a sustainable solution to protect freedom of expression and advance open, safe, and secure access to information, both of which are critical to development of a democratic and open society and a rule of law. Effective technology solutions must be informed by human needs and deployed using approaches that are sensitive to local culture, politics, and human rights history and traumas.

Some specific areas in which the CECC could encourage greater support and development through various existing and expanded U.S. government programs and initiatives include:

- Expanding support **for uncensored multimedia platforms** for Chinese voices and independent news, discussion, and rights-related information, including through creative use of **social networking tools and YouTube**.
- Development and safe dissemination of **circumvention tools** beyond the small group of sophisticated netizens already able to use these tools.
- **Capacity-building initiatives** that more effectively use interactive web-based conference tools to allow a greater range of targeted participants that avoid the expense, travel restrictions, and other political limitations of on-site events.
- Promote diverse, concrete solutions and approaches for **doing business responsibly in China**,[9] including multi-stakeholder initiatives, e.g., encouraging companies to join and help develop the Global Network Initiative. The February 2010 letter from Senator Richard Durbin to 30 technology companies asking them to join the Global Network Initiative and seeking more information about their business practices in China is one welcome step. In light of the global

nature of the challenges, the U.S. should also explore joint initiatives with other governments.

The Google decision announced this week also illustrates the possibility of moving strategically beyond an either/or mentality of stay-and-censor or leave-the-country. By making its most recent move to redirect users from Google.cn to Google.com.hk, and by creating an additional website clearly and regularly updating the status of the Chinese government's interference, Google has contributed to increasing the transparency of and possible accountability for Chinese censorship. Although it's not clear whether this one- country, two systems move will evade the censorship system, at the very least, Google has taken a stand that it will no longer be complicit in Chinese government violation of human rights.

The human rights and business issues and challenges are complex, and as Google co-founder Sergey Brin stated, "The story's not over yet."

Thank you and I look forward to your questions.

End Notes

[1] For more detailed discussion on cyber-espionage, see Ron Deibert and Rafal Rohozinski, "Tracking GhostNet: Investigating a Cyber Espionage Network," Information Warfare Monitor, Munk Centre, JR02-2009, March 29, 2009, *http://www.scribd.com/doc/13731776/* Tracking-GhostNet-Investigating-a-Cyber-Espionage-Network.

[2] See U.S. Congressional-Executive Commission on China, 2009 Annual Report, available at *http://www.cecc.gov/pages/annualRpt/annualRpt09/CECCannRpt2009.pdf*; U.S. Department of State, 2009 Human Rights Report: China (includes Tibet, Hong Kong, and Macau), available at http://www.state.gov/g/drl/rls/hrrpt/2009/eap/135989.htm; United Nations Committee Against Torture, "Concluding observations of the Committee against Torture: China," UN Doc. CAT/C/CHN/CO/4, December 12, 2008, available at http://www2.ohchr.org/english/bodies/cat/cats41.htm; United Nations Committee on the Elimination of Racial Discrimination, "Concluding Observations of the Committee on the Elimination of Racial Discrimination: China," UN Doc. CERD/C/CHN/CO/10-13, August 28, 2009, available at http://www2.ohchr.org/english/bodies/cerd/cerds75.htm. See also HRIC's recent parallel reports to UN bodies: Human Rights in China, *Implementation of the Convention on the Elimination of All Forms of Racial Discrimination in the People's Republic of China: A Parallel NGO Report by Human Rights in China*, June 2009, http://www.hrichina.org/public/PDFs/Reports/2009-CERD_Report.pdf; Human Rights in China, *Implementation of the Convention Against Torture and Other Cruel, Inhuman or Degrading Treatment or Punishment in the People's Republic of China: A Parallel NGO Report by Human Rights in China,* October 2008, *http://hrichina.org/public/PDFs/* Submissions/HRIC-CAT-2008-FINAL.pdf; Human Rights in China, *Implementation and Protection of Human Rights in the People's Republic of China: A Parallel NGO Report by Human Rights in China*, September 2008, *http://hrichina.org/public/PDFs/Submissions/*

2008_HRIC_UPR_Report.pdf (submitted to the UN Human Rights Council in advance of China's 2009 Universal Periodic Review).

3 For more detailed discussion on the Chinese government's tools for suppressing information access and exchange, see Ronald Deibert, *China's Cyberspace Control Strategy: An Overview and Consideration of Issues for Canadian Policy*, February 2010, available at http://www.canadianinternationalcouncil.org; James Fallows, "The Connection Has Been Reset," The Atlantic Monthly, March 2008, *http://www.theatlantic.com/magazine/archive/* 2008/03/-ldquothe-connection-has-been-reset-rdquo/6650/; Andrew Lih, "In Brief: Google's China Move," Andrew Lih Blog, posted on March 23, 2010, http://www.andrewlih.com/blog/2010/03/23/in-brief-googles-china-move/; and Rebecca MacKinnon, "China, the Internet and Google," Rconversation Blog, posted on March 23, 2010, http://rconversation.blogs.com/rconversation/2010/03/china-the-internet-and-google.html.

4 For instance, Article 19 of the Universal Declaration of Human Rights (UDHR) states that "[e]veryone has the right to freedom of opinion and expression; this right includes freedom to hold opinions without interference and to seek, receive and impart information and ideas through any media and regardless of frontiers," while under Article 12, "[n]o one shall be subjected to arbitrary interference with his privacy, family, home or correspondence, nor to attacks upon his honour and reputation. Everyone has the right to the protection of the law against such interference or attacks." UDHR, G.A. res. 217A (III), U.N. Doc A/810 at 71 (1948).

5 Complete English translations of the criminal verdict of the Beijing No. 1 Intermediate People's Court and the decision of the Beijing Municipal High People's Court against Liu Xiaobo have been made available by HRIC in its quarterly publication China Rights Forum, 2010, no. 1, and will soon be made available at *http://www.hrichina.org/public/contents/* category?cid=1043. In addition, English translations of the six articles by Liu Xiaobo that formed the basis of his criminal conviction have been made available by HRIC in the same issue of China Rights Forum; a complete English translation of *Charter 08* has been made available by HRIC at http://www.hrichina.org/public/contents/85717.

6 For more information on these and other individuals, see HRIC's press releases and statements at http://www.hrichina.org/public/contents/category?cid=1052.

7 Presently, two factions within the party, known as the Princeling Faction and the Youth League Faction, are engaged in an intense power struggle. The Princeling Faction has currently seized favorable geopolitical and socioeconomic conditions to gain the upper hand. Their representative, Xi Jinping, is preparing to take over the duties of General Secretary of the CPC from Hu Jintao. Meanwhile, Li Keqiang, the representative of the Youth League Faction, is preparing to take over from Wen Jiabao as the Premier of the State Council. However, much can happen between today and the fall of 2012, and what will happen in the end is still uncertain.

8 Since May 2002, HRIC has submitted 60 individual cases to the WGAD with 17 opinions issued by the WGAD. The conclusion of each and every one of these opinions is that the detention in question is arbitrary, meaning that individuals were being detained for exercising fundamental freedoms or that the circumstances of their detentions violated international standards and norms. The U.S. government should urge action on the part of the Chinese government in these and other cases of arbitrary detention of courageous activists and individuals. By releasing these individuals, China will demonstrate its respect for international human rights and its compliance with the decisions of international human bodies.

9 See Human Rights in China, "Human Rights: Everyone's Business," *China Rights Forum*, 2008, no. 1, http://www.hrichina.org/public/contents/category?cid=164873.

In: Promoting Global Internet Freedom
Editor: Samantha R. Weber
ISBN: 978-1-61728-827-2

Chapter 12

STATEMENT OF ED BLACK, PRESIDENT AND CEO, COMPUTER & COMMUNICATIONS INDUSTRY ASSOCIATION, BEFORE THE CONGRESSIONAL-EXECUTIVE COMMISSION ON CHINA, HEARING ON "GOOGLE AND INTERNET CONTROL IN CHINA: A NEXUS BETWEEN HUMAN RIGHTS AND TRADE?"

Ed Black

Good afternoon. We appreciate the efforts of this Commission and especially Chairmen Dorgan and Levin to address the issue of Internet freedom, and I thank you for the opportunity to testify today. It is an issue that will impact the shape of the world we will live in, especially with regard to trade, privacy and human rights. For too long the U.S. business community has had insufficient support from the U.S. government in responding to other nations' efforts to censor or spy on their citizens, and to interfere with the reasonable flow of services, products, and information. Companies are on the front lines in the battle for Internet freedom, but when they are confronted with foreign government demands, the governments that represent these companies must lead in the defense of Internet freedom and free trade principles.

While I now represent a wide variety of technology and communication companies, I was honored to served in the State and Commerce Departments under five Secretaries in the 1970's, and early 80's, where I worked on East-West trade and was actively involved in the approval of the first U.S./China trade agreement. I later chaired and still serve on the State Department's Advisory Committee on International Communication and Information Policy. The interconnection between trade and human rights, including freedom of expression, is an issue I have seen from various vantage points and have cared deeply about throughout my career.

Our nation founded the Internet. Since that time, our government, and those who are committed to freedom and democracy, should have been out there creating and promoting visionary multilateral understandings designed to maximize freedom on the Internet. We are still at an historic crossroads, and we need to seize the opportunity to ensure the Internet lives up to its potential to spread knowledge, awareness, and expand human potential. If we do not lead, we can expect other governments to stifle or distort that potential.

Over the past decade the Internet has grown into the most efficient tool to communicate, exchange information, spark innovation and extend opportunity to many millions around the world. The Internet platform provides a level playing field for anyone to access information, and it gives disadvantaged people and underrepresented and oppressed groups around the world new opportunities to participate in economic, social, cultural and political activity.

Access to the Internet --- and the ability to fully use it for communication, commerce, and exchanging information --- is more than just a First Amendment issue in this country. The United Nations recognizes freedom of expression as a right. Internet freedom is nothing less than freedom of expression in the 21st century. It must become a top-tier human rights, foreign policy and trade issue.

Freedom and openness are the essence of the Internet, which is what makes it such a powerful communications tool. Totalitarian regimes have depended on tightly controlling the flow of information, both domestically and from the outside world, and they have been increasingly restricting the Internet to maintain their control of information. It is a natural temptation for any government to want to achieve its goals by all means possible. This makes the Internet a tempting target to turn into a tool of state control. But we must protect Internet openness not just from those who want to use it for repression, but also from the many seemingly noble, well-meaning efforts to control specific content or monitor Internet traffic.

Direct challenges to the openness and freedom of the Internet are serious and dangerous. In the long run, though, we may find an equally great threat to Internet freedom will come not from direct attacks, which strike a fatal blow, but from a chipping away of openness – a death by a thousand cuts. This happens as every seemingly well- intentioned effort to remedy a societal problem wins an exception to openness. Repressive regimes use that same technology, and rationale, to filter the Internet or spy for reasons our nation does not support. Our best response to this is for countries who support freedom of expression, non-governmental organizations and consortia like the Global Network Initiative (GNI) to work together to adopt a common ethic of principles for Internet freedom, and to build on that support in whatever form and by whatever means are possible.

My testimony explains that: (a) Internet censorship is a human rights issue and a trade issue; and (b) Internet freedom is a principle that countries purporting to espouse democracy and the welfare of their citizens should practice and protect. Internet freedom must be advanced through leading by example here at home and using negotiations, human rights reports and trade agreements to build international support for Internet freedom principles so as to make outliers of countries that seek to isolate their citizens and use the Internet for censorship, spying and repression.

Censorship is a Human Rights Issue

The Internet can be the greatest tool in history for people to gather information, communicate and provide a more open, transparent relationship between government and its citizens. Or, the Internet can be among the greatest tools for political repression – depending on how it is used. If we fail to take action, others may pervert the Internet and finally bring about the Orwellian future we thought we had avoided, one in which governments perpetually spy, surveil, censor and control - and say they are doing it for our own good.

We fail the citizens of China, Vietnam, Iran and many other Internet-Restricting Countries when we fail to note their governments' censorship[1] and website blocking in human rights reports. For example, in the 2007 Country Reports on Human Rights issued by the State Department, China was upgraded on its human rights issues – despite the apparent increase that year in censorship and surveillance on the Internet.

To respond to government crackdowns on protesters while looking away when a government cracks down on access to the open Internet sends a signal that we are not serious about Internet freedom. The U.S. government must consistently treat Internet freedom as a human rights issue in its dealings and communications with foreign governments.

The need for countries that support freedom of expression to use trade and diplomatic means to exert pressure on Internet censorship is only increasing. Every week we fail to take strong action seems to be viewed as a green light by Internet Restricting Countries like China to further curtail Internet freedom. Last month, China announced new trial restrictions on Internet websites. According to the Associated Press, anyone wanting to start a website in China must now submit identity cards, photos of themselves and meet with Chinese regulators and service provides before they can register their website. The Chinese government claims this will reduce pornography, but it will clearly also crack down on anyone disagreeing with the government online.

We're here today partly because of the high profile battle of a major technology company in China. But the number of companies and countries impacted are far greater. There are few easy answers for companies as they try to bring their technology services and communications tools into nations that have different rules about free speech and freedom of expression. Without the backing of their own government, companies often are faced with the unappealing decision to follow local laws or else exit the market. Staying and engaging can in some cases offer choices to citizens in a repressive country that they wouldn't otherwise have. What companies face varies from country to country. The involvement of the federal government, pushing for a common ethic, can help ease the complexity companies are forced to handle in negotiating operating deals. But the complexity and diversity of situations faced by companies means that rigid statutory solutions may cause unexpected problems and even be counterproductive.

Ultimately countries – not companies -- must battle countries on human rights issues. But companies are working alongside government and human rights groups to support Internet freedom. The Global Network Initiative (GNI) is a collaborative project begun in 2008 in which a handful of American companies, including Microsoft, Google and Yahoo!, participate with international human rights organizations and academics to find productive pathways forward in the quest for Internet freedom and unimpeded commercial market access, being careful not to jeopardize employees or other citizens in Internet Restricting Countries. Key Members of Congress, including Senator Richard Durbin (D-IL) and Rep. Chris Smith (R-NJ), have expressed strong support for GNI and Secretary Clinton did so as well in a major policy address in January. Congress and the Administration should encourage broader participation in the GNI by a wider range of U.S. companies, foreign nations and foreign and multinational corporations.

I have seen China make extraordinary strides through economic engagement with the outside world to the point where it is now one of the most influential economies in the world. However, while a policy of engagement may be a necessary condition for increased freedom, it is not in and of itself sufficient to create freedom. As U.S. companies face pressure from the Chinese government in the course of their business activities in China, support from their own government is needed to ensure that they are not taken advantage of, and that China understands that access to its markets is not a coin that enables them to buy their way out of respecting human rights and freedom. Countries that have supported China's growth as a world player in the belief that its economic growth would lead to its becoming a "responsible stakeholder" need to take a stand when China's unreasonable demands on issues like Internet censorship prove inconsistent with such responsibility.

CENSORSHIP IS A TRADE ISSUE

The United States is an information economy, and U.S. companies are leading vendors of information products and services. In this context, information discrimination by other countries fundamentally undermines U.S. economic interests, including the interests of U.S. companies seeking to access foreign markets, including those engaged in electronic commerce. Filtering American content and services has the effect of filtering American competition, and combating it should top our trade agenda.

The development of the Internet has led to a revolution in the way we conduct international commerce and trade. The success of e-commerce depends on users feeling comfortable and secure enough to utilize the services our industry provides. That comfort and security can only exist in an environment of Internet freedom. When a foreign government stifles online freedom or otherwise restricts the Internet, it creates a hostile market environment by preventing its consumers from fully using new products, applications and services offered by or through U.S. tech companies.

Government restrictions on the Internet affect trade in a variety of ways, including as follows:

- Information discrimination represents a classic "non-tariff trade barrier" (NTB) that U.S. trade policy should dismantle. By attempting to co-opt U.S. businesses into content filtering, offenders create barriers to market entry that would not otherwise exist.
- Information discrimination constitutes an unfair "rule of origin" by filtering out (through a nontransparent process) U.S.-originating content such as certain U.S. domains deemed to be "subversive."
- Information discrimination also violates the fundamental free trade principle of "national treatment" to U.S. services and service providers. This provides a leg up to foreign competitors of U.S. companies, thus allowing U.S. companies to be perceived as being coerced into lowering their corporate moral standards and leading to negative public reaction and even penalties at home.
- The WTO requires transparency and access to judicial or administrative review for measures affecting trade in services. Foreign governments, however, regularly restrict the Internet without transparency and accountability.
- When a country blocks access to a U.S. search engine or website, the advertising on those sites is also being blocked, and trade in the products and services advertized are interfered with. This could particularly impact small businesses that rely on U.S. websites to reach international markets.

If foreign governments push U.S. tech companies out of their domestic market, small businesses that rely on these sites to advertise or directly sell goods would be forced to do business instead with those nations' domestic companies that offer similar services that compete with U.S. companies. Indeed, the unreasonable demands the Chinese government has continuously placed on U.S. companies -- from censorship coercion to Green Dam to Indigenous Innovation -- all seem to have the added objective of clearing the competitive deck of foreign companies.

A special note with respect to China: the Chinese government has been pursuing various "indigenous innovation" policies aimed at controlling technology development and promoting local technology companies. These technology policies extend to the Internet space as well, where Chinese government has been making it difficult for foreign companies to compete and favoring local companies. China's Indigenous Innovation procurement requirement requires Chinese government agencies to purchase only products for which intellectual property was developed and owned in China. Both

Indigenous Innovation and Internet censorship are policies that set the price of access to the Chinese market at an unacceptable level of submissiveness.

The European Union was laudably quick to take the first step to recognize and respond to the issue of Internet freedom as a trade issue. In 2007, the European Parliament overwhelmingly passed a proposal to treat Internet censorship as a trade barrier by a vote of 571 -38. Hopefully, the European Commission will soon take the necessary further action to implement this policy.

First Steps to Promote Internet Freedom

Having neglected to devote appropriate attention to foreign governments' restrictions of Internet content and services, we now have considerable work before us. This is where we should begin:

- The U.S. government should investigate cases of Internet censorship and The United States Trade Representative (USTR), the State Department and Commerce Department should raise issues of Internet restrictions and combat them using the means of their respective offices. Secretary Clinton's major policy speech is an especially noteworthy and commendable beginning. We appreciate actions like the letter the USTR issued in June after China announced all personal computers sold as of July 1 must have the Green Dam Internet filtering software. But our nation has historically missed opportunities to use our existing trade agreements or even reports as leverage in constraining Internet restrictions, censorship, and surveillance.
- USTR should highlight Internet censorship policies in trade reports. In 2006, the USTR issued a report that was billed as a top to bottom review of U.S.-China trade relations. The report discussed simple infringement of intellectual property, yet did not even mention Internet censorship policies. In U.S. government trade reports, more attention needs to be paid to Internet restrictions taken in the name of censorship. Every year, the USTR conducts the Special 301 review, in which we assess our trade relationships with an eye toward intellectual property protection. Do principles of free expression deserve any less protection? If we are willing to make adequate

protection for copyrighted movies a litmus test for our trade relations, how can Internet freedom be worthy of any less?

- In its annual reports on trade barriers, the USTR should review foreign government restrictions on the Internet – taken in the name of censorship or otherwise – and take appropriate action. If it is found that censorship and surveillance impairs U.S. business interests, we should reassess and adjust our trade relationships accordingly.
- Ultimately, the U.S. government should negotiate provisions that promote Internet commerce, openness and freedom in trade and other agreements.
- The U.S. government should use existing trade agreements wherever appropriate to address Internet restrictions.
- The State Department should actively support GNI. It already lends financial support to censorship technology circumvention projects in Internet Restricting Countries. By encouraging broader American corporate responsibility and participation in GNI, and by seeking the participation of our allies abroad such as the European Union, Congress and the State Department could boost GNI's visibility and effectiveness worldwide.
- The potential effectiveness of treating and contesting Internet censorship as a trade barrier lies in the fact that there is a global rules-based system on trade that nations are obligated to follow. A multilateral rules-based approach may create the necessary leverage to make Internet Restricting Countries respect the economic significance of restricting Internet freedom.

Internet Freedom Begins at Home

In addition to using existing trade agreements and human rights monitoring to combat Internet censorship and spying, the United States must lead by example when in comes to Internet freedom and openness by being a model:

We should look at policies enacted by Congress or various government agencies to see if they grow Internet access and increase competition among Internet Access Providers. The competition will help when dealing with another threat to the open Internet – legal or policy changes that allow network level discrimination among end users and messages on the Internet.

We should discourage censorship and surveillance ourselves, restrict intrusive practices such as deep packet inspection and think twice before attempting to block content perceived to be unsavory. Once openness erodes, it's hard to get it back.

We must lead by example. While it is tempting to assume warrantless monitoring of telephone calls, burdensome search engine subpoenas, and regulatory power grabs are not to be equated with the systematic oppression in authoritarian states, these distinctions are hard to make to the rest of the world. To say that our government coerces Internet companies for noble causes while others do so to repress is missing the point: quibbling about the order of magnitude of civilian monitoring will undermine the bold leadership that is necessary to backstop U.S. Internet companies when they are facing down the Thought Police around the world. If our government leads the fight for Internet freedom - by example at home and by negotiations around the world - it will provide invaluable political support to U.S. companies trying to honestly and ethically compete in challenging markets.

CONCLUSION

If the U.S. government and others who value liberty, do not push Internet freedom to the top of the priority list now, they will be failing the future. We are now faced with a "dangerous opportunity". China's policy of coerced censorship has now become a matter of global public concern. The U.S. government should take advantage of this moment by pushing for substantive policies that would not only support U.S. businesses resisting Internet oppression, but would also ensure that no company is left to combat a foreign government's Internet repression on its own. If the U.S. government does not take meaningful action, foreign governments will conclude that they are free to pick off individual companies and intimidate them into submission.

Nations that support human freedom, dignity, and democracy should ensure Internet freedom starts at home and set standards by adopting policies that support a free open Internet. If the Internet is to fulfill its potential as the printing press of the Digital Age, neither a government nor an Internet access provider should act as a gatekeeper, quashing access and content at their whim. At the end of the day, companies can't fight repressive regimes alone on Internet freedom. They need government to lead.

Oppressive foreign governments may not easily change their ways but they need to be made to understand the depth of U.S. and international commitment to Internet openness and freedom. We need to elevate this issue to the top of our diplomatic and trade agenda. Finally, we must be consistent with our own Internet freedom policies and fight for Internet freedom as a common principle so that other nations understand our commitment to curbing censorship of the Internet and threats to Internet freedom in whatever form they manifest.

End Notes

[1] While the policy discussion around Internet-restricting countries often refers to "censorship", there are in fact a variety of practices at issue. When we casually refer to Internet censorship, we must recognize that this includes restrictions such as filtering, blocking, and delaying; state - imposed penalties for posting "wrongthink" online; as well as the self-censorship induced by perpetual state surveillance.

In: Promoting Global Internet Freedom
Editor: Samantha R. Weber ISBN: 978-1-61728-827-2

Chapter 13

TESTIMONY OF AMBASSADOR MARK PALMER, BEFORE THE CONGRESSIONAL - EXECUTIVE COMMISSION ON CHINA, HEARING ON "GOOGLE AND INTERNET CONTROL IN CHINA: A NEXUS BETWEEN HUMAN RIGHTS AND TRADE?"

Mark Palmer

As the father of modern China, Sun Yat-sen once noted: "Worldwide trends are enormous and powerful; those who follow them prosper, and those who resist them perish." The Internet is the most powerful force for progress in our lifetimes. The fact that more than four hundred million Chinese already are online testifies to its enormous importance for China.

At a time when Freedom House, the State Department and others have documented increasing censorship of the Internet, and an overall decline of human rights in China and across the globe, it is easy to become pessimistic about the Internet's prospects. But I believe we need to look more deeply at recent history, at what the Chinese people themselves want, at what we can do to respond to their aspirations and at what the State Department for three years has refused to do.

The single most strategic failure of our best minds in the intelligence, journalist and academic communities over the past half century has been their failure to anticipate, indeed even allow for, peaceful democratic revolution. And yet some sixty such revolutions have occurred in countries as divergent as Indonesia, the Philippines, South Africa, Chile, and Ukraine.

We have neither understood what is going on in the minds of elites beneath the closed surface of dictatorships nor the power of students, women and others once they organize. We now know from his secretly tape-recorded, recently published memoir, that Zhao Ziyang, the General Secretary of the Communist Party of China, ultimately concluded that for China's economic success to continue it must be accompanied by a modern political system with a free press, multiple party elections and an independent judiciary. His predecessor as General Secretary of the Communist Party Hu Yaobang was sacked for heading in the same direction.

Over eleven thousand of the most influential thinkers in China have signed in their own names Charter 08 which explicitly calls for all human rights to be respected and an "end to the practice of viewing words as crimes".

I emphasize elite thinking because of my own experience over forty years of living in and working on European communist countries. While we caught glimpses of their views and debates when they were still in power, I participated in President Reagan's first meetings with General Secretary Gorbachev and was close to the last communist leaders of Hungary, we now understand from numerous documents and interviews how deeply troubled senior and mid-level party officials were with their situations and how often just one man at the top or a small group of elders or security officials held back democratic openings. And I have seen with my own eyes the Iron Curtain coming down across Europe -- something conventional wisdom thought was impossible.

Beyond elites, in China today it is quite extraordinary how many public protests take place every day and across the country, some 90,000 a year according to official statistics. The support for Google's splendid determination to resist censorship of the Internet speaks volumes about the desire of hundreds of millions to enjoy the same access and rights as their colleagues in Taiwan and across the developed world.

While Hu Jintao boasts about his own use of the Internet, he also has called for it to be "purified" and said "Whether we can cope with the Internet is a matter that affects the stability of the state." By which he means the stability of the one-party state. He is keenly aware that both elite and popular opinion, if allowed free rein on the Internet, will bring about the fall of communist dictatorship.

This fear of the Internet, of his own people and elites, has led Hu Jintao to unleash a truly massive program to control and censor the Internet. What can we do to ensure that the Chinese people circumvent these controls, to bring the Great Firewall down and not only in China but Iran and other increasingly repressive countries as well?

Some of the students who were present on Tiananmen Square during the 1989 massacre came to the United States and earned doctoral degrees in computer sciences from leading American universities. They realized the enormous popularity and potential of the Internet in China and were urged by Chinese still in China to find ways to use their computer engineering skills to combat growing censorship and growing overall violations of human rights.

Beginning in 2000 they have developed a system of software and servers, which over the past decade has grown to be the world's largest circumvention system, providing for roughly 90% of anti-censorship traffic in China and worldwide. About a million Chinese and hundreds of thousands of Iranians are frequent users of this system. It works through the distribution of encrypted, secure, free software and by constantly switching IP addresses, up to 10,000 times per hour, on dedicated servers located across the world. They have built and staffed this system with volunteer labor and virtually no financial support from others.

The major limitation on this Global Internet Freedom Consortium's (GIF) ability to serve even much larger numbers of users and to bring down the Firewall altogether is money. They have had to make hard choices between serving a surge in Iranian users last summer and fall and reducing their availability to Chinese users as their servers were crashing. GIF needs to buy many more servers and finally to support fulltime staff. Competing with and staying ahead of over 50,000 heavily financed engineers and censors in China requires a dedicated and properly financed team. We spend $800 million annually on "old media" like VOA and RFA and an additional $1.7 billion on democracy support. Surely we can and should spend $50-100 million per year on a system or systems to circumvent Internet censorship and bring down this firewall.

Realizing the enormous success of this Global Internet Freedom Consortium and its potential, a bipartisan group of Senators and Congressmen appropriated $15 million in 2008 to begin to scale up this system and any others which could demonstrate proven ability to circumvent internet censorship in China, Iran and elsewhere. And in 2010 another $30 million was appropriated.

In my 26 years within the State Department and 20 years outside working on democracy and human rights, I have never been more convinced of the power of any innovation to help those still living in one of the world's 43 remaining dictatorships, half of them Chinese, to liberate themselves.

I also have never been more appalled at the State Department's refusal to do what is so clearly in the national interest of the United States. In flagrant and now repeated violation of Congressional legislation, the State Department has refused to use the appropriated funds to scale up an existing, successful circumvention system. State Department staff- level officials have made a mockery first of Secretary Rice's and now Secretary Clinton's frequently voiced and sincere commitments to help ensure freedom of the Internet.

Let us take just one dimension of American national interest. There is a profoundly false understanding of the Google-China issue -- as if Google must lose its China market because it no longer accepts Google.cn censorship. If the United States acts in the manner we seek, and people in China can access Google.com, sell Baidu stock short. And watch Google pick up support from Iran, Syria, and elsewhere. Google's in a fight and a martyred defeat will not help the cause. It too should be pressing the State Department and working with GIF. If it does so, its franchise throughout the world will be enhanced by orders of magnitude for being not merely a wounded victim but the provider of enhanced closed society access to the Internet.

Fortunately key members of Congress are determined that the State Department finally does the right thing. Senators Brownback, Casey, Kaufman, Kyl and Specter, three Democrats and two Republicans, wrote to Secretary Clinton on January 20, 2010. After expressing concern that the State Department's use of the FY08 funds "did not materially enhance Internet access", they stressed that "the FY10 Consolidated Appropriations Act requires as a matter of law that the Internet Freedom funds be awarded applicants who currently and demonstrably are able to expand Internet access to 'large numbers of users living in closed societies that have acutely hostile Internet environments. The intent of this language is clear: funds should facilitate immediate and order-of-magnitude scale- ups of proven, field-tested protocols that facilitate access to the Internet by pro- democracy demonstrators in Iran, China, and elsewhere".

To get the State Department's attention, two weeks ago Senator Brownback put a hold on the confirmation of four ambassadorial and assistant secretary nominations. At a press conference on March 18th, the Senator citing renewed State Department interest removed these holds. But he stressed "the objective is clear, and delay is the chief ingredient of the problem. The funds must be rapidly dispersed to groups that possess the current capability of immediately opening access to the Internet for millions of new users. One such group is the Global Internet Freedom Consortium, which operates the Freegate circumvention system relied upon by millions around the world. If there are others that can fulfill these criteria, then the State Department should come forward with clear and convincing evidence and we should support those groups as well."

Senator Brownback continued "But we must act now. If we do not achieve a breakthrough in the next week, I will not hesitate to place holds on future State Department nominations for as long as it takes to move the Department away from policies that will keep the firewalls in business for years." Senator Kyl also spoke at the March 18th press conference, affirmed that he shared Senator Brownback's assessment and will join in future holds.

We strongly urge the Congressional-Executive Commission on China also to press the State Department to move promptly to work out an agreed strategy with concerned members of Congress.

We all agree that it is profoundly in our interest for the Chinese people to have direct and uncensored access to the Internet, that the censorship be circumvented and ultimately defeated. We have it in our power to achieve this goal. Further delay will be an act of moral cowardice and a failure of strategic vision.

In: Promoting Global Internet Freedom ISBN: 978-1-61728-827-2
Editor: Samantha R. Weber

Chapter 14

Testimony of Rebecca MacKinnon, Visiting Fellow, Center for Information Technology Policy, Princeton University, before the Congressional-Executive Commission on China, Hearing on "Google and Internet Control in China: A Nexus between Human Rights and Trade?"

Rebecca MacKinnon

Thank you for the opportunity to submit this testimony for the record. I am Rebecca MacKinnon, a visiting fellow at Princeton University's Center for Technology Policy. From 1992-2001, for more than nine years, I worked as a journalist for CNN in China. For the last six years while based at several different academic institutions I have researched Chinese Internet censorship alongside global censorship trends, examining in particular how the private sector assists government efforts to silence or manipulate citizen speech. I am a founding member of the Global Network Initiative, a nongovernmental multi-stakeholder initiative that aims to help Internet and telecommunications companies uphold the principles of free expression and privacy around the world. I am also co-founder of an international bloggers' network called

Global Voices Online. Several of our contributors regularly summarize and translate conversations from the Chinese blogosphere, and report on developments related to online free expression in China. My testimony today is informed by my experience as a journalist who has lived under Chinese censorship and surveillance; as a researcher of Chinese Internet censorship; as a practitioner of new media and participant in Chinese- language online communities; and as an advocate for free expression and human rights on the Internet.th

On January 12th Google stunned the world with its dramatic announcement that it was reconsidering its business in China in the wake of debilitating cyber-attacks, and furthermore that the company was no longer willing to continue operating a censored[1] Search 22nd engine in China, Google.cn, launched in January 2006. On March, Google redirected Google.cn to the Hong Kong-based search engine Google.com.hk, where it now provides uncensored search results in the simplified character set used by people in Mainland China.[2] In my testimony, I will briefly describe the context of the Google decision. I will then outline some of the different tactics used by the Chinese government to censor and control online speech, including tactics used against Google. I will describe what some Chinese citizens are doing in order to evade and oppose these tactics. Finally, I will offer some specific policy suggestions for how the United States can help to improve Internet freedom in China.

The Context of Google's China Announcement

American Internet company executives have long argued that more connectivity will bring more freedom - even in repressive regimes where the Internet is under heavy censorship and surveillance. Statements to that effect were a common theme in Congressional testimony given by Google and Yahoo executives at the February 2006 hearing convened by the late Rep. Tom Lantos.[3] Since then, Chinese Internet usage has nearly quadrupled. Stories abound of how Internet users in China have helped expose corruption, bring justice to innocent victims of official malfeasance, and even change some laws and regulations. But this has not changed the regime's repressive attitude toward dissent. According to a recent report by the Dui Hua Foundation, in 2008 arrests and indictments on charges of "endangering state security" – the most common charge used in cases of political, religious, or ethnic dissent – more than doubled for the second time in th ree years.[4]

China is pioneering a new kind of Internet-age authoritarianism. It is demonstrating how a non-democratic government can stay in power while simultaneously expanding domestic Internet and mobile phone use. In China today there is a lot more give-and-take between government and citizens than in the pre-Internet age, and this helps bolster the regime's legitimacy with many Chinese Internet users who feel that they have a new channel for public discourse. Yet on the other hand, as this Commission's 2009 Annual Report clearly outlined, Communist Party control over the bureaucracy and courts has strengthened over the past decade, while the regime's institutional commitments to protect the universal rights and freedoms of all its citizens have weakened.[5]

Google's public complaint about Chinese cyber-attacks and censorship occurred against this backdrop. It reflects a recognition that China's *status quo* – at least when it comes to censorship, regulation, and manipulation of the Internet – is unlikely to improve any time soon, and may in fact continue to get worse.

Overview of Chinese Internet Controls

Chinese government attempts to control online speech began in the late 1990's with a focus on the filtering or "blocking" of Internet content. Today, the government deploys an expanding repertoire of tactics. They include: deletion or removal of content at the source, device and local-level controls, domain name controls, localized disconnection or restriction, self-censorship due to surveillance, cyber-attacks, government "astro-turfing," local government "outreach," and targeted police intimidation.

- **Filtering or "blocking:"** This is the original and best understood form of Internet censorship. Internet users on a particular network are blocked from accessing specific websites. The technical term for this kind of censorship is "filtering." Some congressional proceedings and legislation have also referred to this kind of censorship as "Internet jamming." Filtering can range in scope from a home network, a school network, university network, corporate network, the entire service of a particular commercial Internet Service Provider (ISP), or all Internet connections within a specific country. It is called "filtering" because a network administrator uses special software or hardware to block access to specified web pages by banning access to certain designated domain names, Internet addresses, or any page containing specified keywords or phrases. A wide range of commercial filtering products are developed and marketed here in the United States by U.S. companies for filtering by parents, schools, government departments, businesses, and anybody else who wants to control how their networks are used. All Internet routers – including those manufactured by the U.S. company Cisco Systems – come with the ability to filter because it is necessary for basic cyber-security and blocking universally reviled content like child pornography. However, the same technology can just as easily be used to block political content. According to the Open Net Initiative (ONI), an academic consortium that has been following global Internet filtering since 2002, more than forty countries now practice Internet filtering to some extent at the national level. However China's Internet filtering system – known to many as "the Great[6] Firewall of China" – is the most sophisticated and extensive in the world.In its 2009 report on Chinese Internet censorship, the ONI described increasingly pervasive and sophisticated filtering tactics. "In fine-tuning this system," the report concluded, "China is also adopting subtler and more fluid controls."[7]

- **Deletion and removal of content:** Filtering is the primary means of censoring content over which the Chinese government has no jurisdiction. When it comes to websites and Internet services over which Chinese authorities do have legal jurisdiction – usually because at least some of the company's operations and computer servers are located in-country – why merely block or filter content when you can delete it from the Internet entirely? In Anglo-European legal parlance, the legal mechanism used to implement such a system is called "intermediary liability." The Chinese government calls it "self-discipline," but it amounts to the same thing, and it is precisely the legal mechanism through which Google's Chinese search engine, Google.cn, was required to censor its search results.[8] All Internet companies operating within Chinese jurisdiction – domestic or foreign –are held liable for everything appearing on their search engines, blogging platforms, and social networking services. They are also legally responsible for everything their users discuss or organize through chat clients and messaging services. In this way, much of the censorship and surveillance work is delegated and outsourced by the government to the private sector – who, if they fail to censor and monitor their users to the government's satisfaction, will lose their business license and be forced to shut down. It is also the mechanism through which China-based companies must monitor and censor the conversations of more than fifty million Chinese bloggers. Politically sensitive postings are deleted or blocked from ever being published. Bloggers who get too influential in the wrong ways can have their accounts shut down and their entire blogs erased. That work is done primarily not by "Internet police" but by employees of Internet companies.[9]

- **Cyber-attacks:** The sophisticated, military-grade cyber-attacks launched against Google were targeted specifically at GMail accounts of human rights activists who are either from China or work on China-related issues. This serves as an important reminder that governments and corporations are not the only victims of cyber-warfare and cyber-espionage. Human rights activists, whistleblowers and dissidents around the world, most of whom lack training or resources to protect themselves, have over the past few years been victim of increasingly aggressive cyber attacks.[10] The effect in some cases is either to bring down overseas dissident websites at critical political moments, or causing frequent outages, putting great strain on the site's operators just to keep it running. Websites run by Chinese exiles, dissidents, and human rights defenders have seen increasingly aggressive attacks over the past few years.[11] In other cases the effect is to compromise activists' internal computer networks and e-mail accounts to the point that it becomes too risky to use the Internet at all for certain kinds of organizing and communications, because the dissidents don't feel confident that any of their digital communications are secure. Journalists who report on human rights issues and academics whose research includes human rights problems have also found themselves under aggressive att ack in places like China, exposing their sources and making it much more risky to work on politically sensitive topics. Like the activists, these groups are unprepared and unequipped to deal with cyber - attacks.[12]

- **Device-level and local controls:** In late spring of 2009 the Ministry of Industry and Information Technology (MIIT) mandated that by July 1st of that year all computers sold in China must be pre-installed with a specific software product called "Green Dam – Youth Escort."[13] While the purpose of "Green Dam" was ostensibly for child protection, researchers inside and outside of China quickly uncovered the fact that it not only censored additional political and religious content, it also logged user activity and sent this information back to a central computer server belonging to the software developer's company. [14] The software had other problems which made it easy for U.S. industry to oppose: It contained serious programming flaws which increased the user's vulnerability to cyber -attack. It also violated the intellectual property rights of a U.S. company's filtering product. Faced with uniform opposition from the U.S. computer industry and strong protests from the U.S. government, the MIIT backed down on the eve of its deadline, making the installation of Green Dam voluntary instead of mandatory.[15] The defeat of Green Dam, however, did not diminish other efforts to control and track Internet user behavior at more localized levels within the national "Great Firewall" system – for instance at the level of a school, university, or apartment block as well as at the level of a city-wide Internet Service Provider (ISP). It was reported in September last year that local governments were mandating the use of censoring and surveillance products with names like "Blue Shield" and "Huadun." The function and purpose of these products appeared similar to Green Dam, though they had the benefit of involving neither the end user nor foreign companies.[16] The implementation of these systems has received little attention outside of China.

- **Domain name controls:** In December, the government-affiliated China Internet Network Information Center (CNNIC) announced that it would no longer allow individuals to register Internet domain names ending in .cn. Only companies or organizations be able to use .cn domain.[17] While authorities explained that this measure was aimed at cleaning up pornography, fraud, and spam, a group of Chinese webmasters protested that it also violated individual rights.[18] Authorities announced that more than 130,000 websites had shut down in the cleanup. In January a Chinese newspaper reported that self -employed individuals and freelancers conducting online business had been badly hurt by the measure.[19] Later in February, CNNIC backtracked somewhat, announcing that individuals will once again be allowed to register .cn domains, but all applicants must appear in person to confirm their registration, show a government ID, and submit a photo of themselves with their application.[20] This eliminates the possibility of anonymous domain name registration under .cn and makes it easier for authorities to warn or intimidate website operators when "objectionable" content appears.

- **Localized disconnection and restriction:** In times of crisis when the government wants to ensure that people cannot use the Internet or mobile phones to organize protests, connections are shut down entirely or heavily restricted in specific locations. There have been anecdotal reports of Internet connections going down or text-messaging services suddenly not working in counties or towns immediately after local disturbances broke out. The most extreme case however is Xinjiang province, a traditionally Muslim region bordering Pakistan, Kazakhstan, and Afghanistan in China's far Northwest. After ethnic riots took place in July of last year, the Internet was cut off in the entire province for six months, along with most mobile text messaging and international phone service. Nobody in Xinjiang could send e-mail or access any website – domestic or foreign. Businesspeople had to travel to the bordering province of Gansu just to communicate with customers.[21] Internet access and phone service have now been restored, but with severe limitations on the number of text messages people can send on their mobile phones per day, no access to overseas websites, and even very limited access to domestic Chinese websites. Xinjiang-based Internet users can only access specially watered-down versions of official Chinese news and information sites, with many of the functions such as blogging or comments disabled.[22]

- **Self-censorship due to surveillance:** Surveillance of Internet and mobile users is conducted in a variety of ways, contributing to an atmosphere of self-censorship. Surveillance enables authorities to warn and harass Internet users either via electronic communications or in person when individuals are deemed to be taking their online activities too far. Occasional detention, arrest, or imprisonment of select individuals serves as an effective warning to others that they are being watched. Surveillance techniques include:

- *"Classic" monitoring:* While Chinese surveillance measures are explained by the government to the public as anti-terrorism measures, they are also broadly used to identify, then harass or imprison peaceful critics of the regime. Cybercafes – the cheaper and more popular option for students and less affluent people – are required to monitor users in multiple ways including ID registration upon entry to the café or upon login, surveillance cameras, and monitoring software installed on computers. Surveillance in Chinese cybercafes is known to be so extensive that people who are likely to engage in political conversations online avoid doing so in such facilities.
- *"Law enforcement compliance:"* In a country like China where "crime" is defined broadly to include political dissent, companies with in-country operations and user data stored locally can easily find themselves complicit in the surveillance and jailing of political dissidents. The most notorious example of law enforcement compliance gone badly wrong was when Yahoo's local Beijing staff gave Chinese police account information of journalist Shi Tao, activist Wang Xiaoning, and at least two others engaged in political dissent.[23] There are other examples of how law enforcement compliance by foreign companies has compromised activists.

In 2006, Skype partnered with a Chinese company to provide a localized version of its service, then found itself being used by Chinese authorities to track and log politically sensitive chat sessions by users inside China.[24] This happened because Skype delegated law enforcement compliance to its local partner without sufficient attention to how the compliance was being carried out. China's more sophisticated and politically aware Internet users have long assumed that Chinese -branded e-mail and chat services monitor their communications and share them readily with authorities. As news about these incidents involving foreign -branded products spread among Chinese Internet users, however, many no longer feel that they can trust foreign brands either. They feel they have no choice but to minimize the extent to which they use any Internet or mobile service for politically sensitive conversations for fear that anything and everything might be compromised.

- **Pro-active measures: "astro-turfing" and outreach:** The government increasingly combines censorship and surveillance measures with pro -active efforts to steer online conversations in the direction it prefers. In 2008 the Hong Kong-based researcher David Bandurski determined that at least 280,000 people had been hired at various levels of government to work as "online commentators." Known derisively as the "fifty cent party," these people are paid to write postings that show their employers in a favorable light in online chat rooms, social networking services, blogs, and comments sections of news websites.[25] Many more people do similar work as volunteers – recruited from among the ranks of retired officials as well as college students in the Communist Youth League who aspire to become Party members. This approach is similar to a tactic known as "astro-turfing" in American parlance, now commonly used by commercial advertising firms, public relations companies, and election campaigns around the world.[26] In many provinces it is now also standard practice for government officials – particularly at the city and county level – to work to co-opt and influence independent online writers by throwing special conferences for local bloggers, or inviting them to special press events or news conferences about issues of local concern.[27]

All of these measures are implemented in the context of the Chinese government's broader policies on information and news control. In December the Committee to Protect Journalists listed China as the world's top jailer ofjournalists.[28]

Citizen Pushback

Despite the government's formidable array of control tactics, China's determined, creative, and opinionated Internet users have managed to make the Chinese Internet a lively, fun, and often contentious place.[29] Over the past six years I have been involved with a number of Chinese blogger groups, mailing lists, and social networks. Chinese "netizens" – as they call themselves – are doing a range of things to oppose Internet controls:

- **Informal anti-censorship support networks:** I have attended gatherings of bloggers and journalists in China – with varying degrees of organization or spontaneousness – where participants devoted significant amounts of time to teaching one anoth er how to use circumvention tools to access blocked websites. Informal "teach-ins" on how to access Twitter are especially popular among people who want access to an uncensored, international community of conversation. Certain bloggers are known to post information about how to circumvent censorship and welcome their friends to copy and re-post their work as widely as possible. I have seen numerous Powerpoints presentations and PDF documents containing instruction manuals on how to use various tools, circulated by e-mail or through peer-to-peer instant messaging clients.

- **Distributed web-hosting assistance networks:** I am aware of people who have strong English language and technical skills, as well as overseas credit cards, who are helping friends and acqua intances in China to purchase inexpensive space on overseas web hosting services, then set up independent blogs using free open- source software. The objective is to help people who don't have the technical skills to run a website on their own to avoid a) b eing victim of content removal if they use domestic services, or b) being blocked if they use popular international blogging platforms like Blogspot, Typepad, Livejournal, or Wordpress.com, all of which are blocked in China. Sometimes the people doing this largely volunteer work also help bloggers to switch domain names and IP addresses when the blog gains attention and gets blocked by the "great firewall."

- **Crowdsourced "opposition research:"** With the Chinese government's Green Dam censorware edict last year, we have seen the emergence of loosely organized "opposition research" networks. Last June a group of Chinese computer programmers and bloggers collectively wrote a report exposing Green Dam's political and religious censorship, along with many of its security flaws. They posted the document at Wikileaks.[30] Another anonymous group of Chinese netizens have collected a list of companies and organizations – domestic and foreign – who have helped build China's Internet censorship system.[31]

- **Preservation and relay of censored content:** I have noticed a number of people around the Chinese blogosphere and in chatrooms who make a regular habit of immediately downloading interesting articles, pictures, and videos which they think have a chance of being blocked or removed. They then re-post these materials in a variety of places, and relay them to friends through social networks and e-mail lists.

- **Humorous "viral" protests:** In 2009, Internet censorship tightened considerably. Many lively blogging platforms and social networks where heated political discussions were known to take place were shut down under the guise of an anti -porn crackdown. In response, an anonymous Shanghai-based jokester created an online music video called "Ode to the Grass Mud Horse" – whose technically innocent lyrics, sung by a children's chorus over video of alpaca sheep, contained a string of highly obscene homonyms. The video spawned an entire genre of anti-censorship jokes and videos involving mythical animals whose names sound similar to official slogans and obscenities of various kinds.[32] This viral pranksterism created an outlet for people to vent about censorship, poke fun at the government, and raise awareness among many people who are not comfortable discussing such matters in a direct way.

- **Public persuasion efforts:** A number of prominent liberal Chinese intellectuals and journalists occasionally write essays on personal blogs in which they criticize the government's censorship and information control policies as counterproductive: censorship, they argue, stifles the Chinese people's innovation and creativity, contributes to corruption and economic inefficiency, and generally prevents the nation from fulfilling its real potential. Such arguments have failed to influence government policies in any kind of meaningful way, although individual officials and business leaders sometimes do echo these sentiments in public fora.[33]

It remains unclear when or whether this line of argument will eventually convince China's leadership to relax information controls. The good news, however, is that in China today it is at least possible to make this argument.

Recommendations

Because the Chinese government deploys an expanding range of tactics to control online speech, efforts to promote Internet freedom in China should be similarly multi-pronged and multi-faceted. China's Internet users are pushing back against the controls in a range of ways, as I have described. It is thus important to support, encourage, and enable a range of efforts aimed at tackling different parts of the problem. Finally, corporate social responsibility is essential: It will be much more difficult for Chinese Internet users to fight for their rights if the international business community assists the Chinese government in finding more effective means to muzzle them.

- **Anti-censorship tools:** Congress is to be commended for giving both moral and financial support to programmers who are working hard to develop anti-censorship technologies. In spite of this, I have never ceased to be amazed by the number of university students, academics, journalists, and other white-collar professionals I've encountered on frequent trips to China over the past few years who profess little or no knowledge of circumvention tools and techniques. While no survey data exists to shed light on what percentage of Chinese Internet users know how to circumvent censorship – or are interested in doing so even if they know how – the anecdotal evidence I have gathered leads me to concluded that the percentage must be relatively small, and concentrated among elite groups of tech-savvy people who work in the Internet industry, followers of banned religious groups, and politically active people. The broader Internet-using public in China appears to be largely in the dark about how to access blocked websites. Funding for software development, therefore, needs to be accompanied by equally robust support for education and outreach among broader segments of Chinese society beyond the obvious communities.

- **Anonymity and security tools:** In my interactions with Chinese journalists, human rights, lawyers, bloggers, and academics, I've found that most of them are shockingly uneducated about how to evade online surveillance, how to secure their e-mail, how to detect and eliminate spyware on their computers, and how to guard against even the most elementary cyber-attacks. Chinese-language, culturally appropriate technologies, accompanied by robust education and training, is badly needed. The recent attacks against Chinese GMail users only highlights the urgency.

- **Capture, preservation, and distribution of censored content:** As I mentioned earlier, a lot of Chinese Internet users are downloading and preserving content before it gets censored, but in an ad-hoc and unorganized way. A searchable, accessible, and secure repository of such materials would be invaluable if somebody had the time, funds, and technical support to create one.

- **Support for "opposition research":** To date, ad-hoc groups conducting research aimed at exposing details of Chinese censorship policies rely primarily on two platforms to publish their findings: Google Documents and Wikileaks.org. It is unclear whether Google Documents will remain accessible in China if Google shuts down Google.cn and reduces or closes its China operations. Wikileaks.org faces bandwith problems and financial difficulties resulting in frequent inaccessibility. Chinese opposition researchers could use help in finding secure, reliable, and accessible platforms through which their work can be disseminated.

- **Corporate responsibility:** To ensure that American Internet businesses in China assume the appropriate level of responsibility for the human rights of their users and customers, I support a voluntary component backed up by legislation if necessary.

    - *Global Network Initiative:* In 2008 Google, Yahoo, and Microsoft took the important step ofjoining the Global Network Initiative (GNI), a code of conduct for free expression and privacy for companies in the Information &Communications Technologies (ICT) sector.[34] The GNI can help companies uphold a shared commitment to the values of free expression and privacy while recognizing that no market is without political difficulties or ethical dilemmas. Just as companies have a social responsibility not to pollute the environment or exploit twelve-year-olds, American companies have a responsibility not to collaborate with the suppression of peaceful speech. The GNI's philosophy is grounded in the belief that people in all markets stand to benefit from Internet and mobile technologies. In most cases companies can still do a lot of good by being engaged in countries whose governments practice at least one of the forms of Internet controls I have described above – as long as they are aware of the human rights implications of their business and technical decisions. It is reasonable to expect all Internet and telecommunications companies to include human rights risk assessments in their decisions about market entry and product development, just as they and other companies consider environmental risks and labor concerns. With a multi-stakeholder membership including human rights groups, socially responsible investors and academics like myself, GNI's goal is to help companies do the right thing while bringing expanded Internet communications and mobile access to the people who stand to benefit from this connectivity the most.

1. The principles' implementation guidelines and accountability framework can be adapted to a range of business models, including hardware companies and Internet service providers if these companies choose to engage with the GNI. As this Commission is aware, Senator Dick Durbin has written to thirty companies urging them to join the GNI and we look forward to working with them so that it will be pos sible for them to join in the near future. While GNI is presently most relevant to Yahoo, Google and Microsoft because those were the three companies that launched the initiative, it is also apparent that the thirty companies contacted by Senator Durbin share varying degrees of human rights risk, even as their business models, technologies, and geographies vary widely. They have an obligation to at least consider joining the GNI and if they choose not to, to find other appropriate policy and operational responses to address the inescapable human rights implications of their products or services.

- *Legislation* – While recognizing that no connectivity at all is even worse than censored connectivity, and also recognizing that many information communications technologies have "dual use" capabilities that can be used for security and legitimate law enforcement as well as repression, it should nonetheless be made more difficult for U.S. companies to provide censorship and surveillance capabilities to Chinese government entities and their corporate affiliates, given the regime's clear track record of using those technologies to suppress peaceful political dissent. It is important, however, that legislation be flexible enough to accommodate the rapidly- changing nature of information communications technology, as well as the complex and highly diverse nature of ICT businesses – including many small startups, as well as innovations that are difficult to define, categorize, or predict in advance. It is also important that any law concerning the human rights implications of ICTs be truly global in scope, recognizing that ICT companies can face human rights dilemmas in almost every market, whether the government involved is technically categorized as "democratic" or "authoritarian."

- *Legal support for victims:* Companies will have a further disincentive to collaborate with repressive surveillance and censorship if victims or corporate collaboration in human rights abuses can more easily sue them in a United States court of law.

- *Incentives for socially responsible innovation:* Companies should be encouraged to develop technologies and service features that enhance users' ability to evade censorship and surveillance, and to help users better understand what personal information is being stored and how it is used.

CONCLUSION

Many of China's nearly 400 million Internet users are engaged in passionate debates about their communities' problems, public policy concerns, and their nation's future. Unfortunately these public discussions are skewed, blinkered, and manipulated – thanks to political censorship and surveillance. The Chinese people are proud of their nation's achievements and generally reject critiques by outsiders even if they agree with some of them. A democratic alternative to China's Internet-age authoritarianism will only be viable if it is conceived and built by the Chinese people from within. In helping Chinese "netizens" conduct an un-manipulated and un -censored discourse about their future, the United States will not imposing its will on the Chinese people, but rather helping the Chinese people to take ownership over their own future.

End Notes

[1] *A new approach to China,* by David Drummond,The Official Google Blog, Jan. 12, 2010, at: http://googleblog.blogspot.com/2010/01/new-approach-to-china.html.

[2] *A new approach to China: an update*, by David Drummond, The Official Google Blog, March 22, 2010 at: http://googleblog.blogspot.com/2010/03/new-approach-to-china-update.html

[3] Testimony of Google Inc. before the Subcommittee on Asia and the Pacific, and the Subcommittee on Africa, Global Human Rights, and International Operations, Committee on International Relations, United States House of Representatives, February 15, 2006, by Elliot Schrage, Vice President, Global Communications and Public Affairs, Google Inc., at: http://googleblog.blogspot.com/2006/02/testimony-internet and Testimony of Michael Callahan, Senior Vice President and General Counsel, Yahoo! Inc., Before the Subcommittees on Africa, Global Human Rights and International Operations, and Asia and the Pacific, February 15, 2006, at: http://yhoo.client.shareholder.com/press/ReleaseDetail.cfm?ReleaseID=1 87725

[4] "Chinese State Security Arrests, Indictments Doubled in 2008," *Dui Hua Human Rights Journal*, March 25, 2009, at: http://www.duihua.org/hrjournal/2009/03/chinese-state-security - arrests.html

[5] 2009 Annual Report, Congressional -Executive Commission on China, at: http://www.cecc.gov/pages/annualRpt/annualRpt09/CECCannRpt2009.pdf

[6] See *Access Denied: The Practice and Policy of Global Internet Filtering* by Diebert, et.al. (MIT Press, 2008). Updates and new country reports are posted regularly at the Open Net Initiative web site at: http://opennet.net

[7] "China" research profile by Stephanie Wang, Open Net Initiative, published on June 15, 2009 at: http://opennet.net/research/profiles/china

[8] See *Race To the Bottom: Corporate Complicity in Chinese Internet Censorship* by Human Rights Watch (August 2006), at http://www.hrw.org/reports/2006/china0806/. Also "Search Monitor Project: Toward a Measure of Transparency," by Nart Villen euve, Citizen Lab Occasional Paper, No.1, University of Toronto (June 2008) at *http://www.citizenlab.org/papers/searchmonitor.pdf*

[9] For more details see "China's Censorship 2.0: How companies censor bloggers," by Rebecca MacKinnon, First Monday (February 2006) at: http://firstmonday.org/htbin/cgiwrap/bin/ojs/index.php/fm/article/view/2378/2089; and "The Chinese Censorship Foreigners Don't See," by Rebecca MacKinnon, The Wall Street Journal Asia, August 14, 2008, at: *http://online.wsj.com/article/SB121865176983837575.html*

[10] See *Tracking Ghostnet: Investigating a Cyber Espionage Network*, by Information War Monitor (March 2009) at http://www.nartv.org/mirror/ghostnet.pdf

[11] "Chinese human rights sites hit by DDoS attack," by Owen Fletcher, *ComputerWorld*, January 26, 2010, at: http://www.computerworld.in/articles/chinese -human -rights -sites-hit-ddos-attack

[12] "National Day triggers censorship, cyber attacks in China," Committee to Protect Journalists, September 22, 2009 at: http://cpj.org/2009/09/national-day-triggers-censorship -cyber-attacksin.php

[13] "China Squeezes PC Makers," by Loretta Chao, *The Wall Street Journal,* June 8, 2009, at: http://online.wsj.com/article/SB124440211524192081.html

[14] *China's Green Dam: The Implications of Government Control Encroaching on the Home PC*, Open Net Initiative bulletin (June, 2009) at: http://opennet.net/chinas-green-dam-the-implications-government Analysis of the Green Dam Censorware System, by Scott Wolchok, Randy Yao, and J. Alex Halderman, Computer Science and Engineering Division, The University of Michigan, June 11, 2009, at: *http://www.cse.umich.edu/%7Ejhalderm/pub/gd/.*

[15] "After the Green Dam Victory," by Rebecca MacKinnon, *CSIS Freeman Report* , June/July 2009, at: http://csis.org/files/publication/fr09n0607.pdf

[16] "China Clamps Down on Internet Ahead of 60th Anniversary," by Owen Fletcher, IDG News Service, September 25, 2009 at: http://www.pcworld.com/article/172627/china_clamps_down_on_internet_ rsary.html ; and "China: Blue Dam activated," by Oiwan Lam, *Global Voices Advocacy*, September 13, 2009 at: http://advocacy.

[17] "China tightens control on domain name registration," by Zhao Chunzhe, China Daily, December 14, 2009, at: http://www.chinadaily.com.cn/china/2009-12/14/content _9174767.htm

[18] "China: Online protest against CNNIC," by Oiwan Lam, *Global Voices Advocacy*, December 22, 2009 at: http://advocacy.

[19] "China: More than 100 thousand websites shut down," by Oiwan Lam, *Global Voices Advocacy,* February 3, 2010, at: http://advocacy. 00-thousand-web sites-shut-down/

[20] "China Further Tightens Rules for Domain Name Owners," by Owen Fletcher, PC World, February 23, 2010, at: http://www.pcworld.com/article/190013/china_further_tightens_rules_for_domain_name_o wners .html

[21] "What Internet? China region cut off 6 months now," by Cara Anna, Associated Press via Yahoo! News, January 19, 2010, at: http://news.yahoo.com/s/ap/20100119/ap_on_bi_ge/as_china_internet

[22] "Blogger describes Xinjiang as an 'internet prison'," Josh Karamay, BBC News, February 3, 2010, at: http://news.bbc.co.uk/2/hi/asia-pacific/8492224.stm

[23] For detailed analysis of the Yahoo! China case see "Shi Tao, Yahoo!, and the lessons for corporate social responsibility," working paper presented at presented December 2007 at the International Conference on Information Technology and Social Responsibility, Chinese University, Hong Kong, at: http://rconversation.blogs

[24] *Breaching Trust,* by Nart Villeneuve, Information Warfare Monitor and ONI Asia Joint Report (October 2008), at: http://www.nartv.org/mirror/breachingtrust.pdf

[25] "China's Guerilla War for the Web,Óby David Bandurski, *Far Eastern Economic Review*, July 2008, at: http://www.feer.com/essays/2008/august/chinas-guerrilla-war

[26] "Astroturfing describes the posting of supposedly independent messages on Internet boards by interested companies and individuals In American politics, the term is used to describe formal public relations projects which deliberately give the impression that they are spontaneous and populist reactio ns. The term comes from Astro Turf-- the fake grass used in many indoor American football stadiums. The contrast between truly spontaneous or "grassroots" efforts and an orchestrated public relations campaign, is much like the distinction between real grass and Astro Turf." From *http://www.answers.com/ topic/astroturfing*

[27] "How China polices the internet,Óby Kathrin Hille, *Financial Times*, July 17, 2009 at: http://www.ft.com/cms/s/2/e716cfc6-7 1 a1-11 de-a82 1-001 44feabdc0.html

[28] "2009 Prison Census," Committee to Protect Journalists, (as of December 1, 2009) at: http://cpj.org/imprisoned/2009.php

[29] For an excellent portrayal of Chinese Internet culture and its contentious, playful nature see *The Power of the Internet in China: Citizen Activism Online* by Guobin Yang, (Columbia University Press, 2009).

[30] "A technical analysis of the Chinese "Green Dam Youth Escort" censorship software," posted June 2009 on Wikileaks.org at: http://wikileaks.org/wiki/A_technical_analysis_of_the_Chinese_%27Green_Dam_Youth-Escort%27 _censorship _software (At time of writing the page cannot be reached due to bandwith and funding problems at Wikileaks.org)

[31] "GFW Engineering Team Name List," posted to Google Documents in January 2010 at: http://docs.google 32"A Dirty Pun Tweaks China's Online Censors,"by Michael Wines, *The*

New York Times, March 11, 2009, at: *http://www.nytimes.com/2009/03/12/world/asia/12beast.html*

[32] "Charles Zhang: Without Reform There is No Way Out"by Xiao Qiang, *China Digital Times*, February 4, 2010, at: http://chinadigitaltimes.net/2010/02/charles-zhang- %E5%BC%A0%E6%9C%9D%E9%98%B3%EF%BC%9Awithout-reform-there-is-no-way-out/

[33] See http://globalnetworkinitiative.org

CHAPTER SOURCES

The following chapters have been previously published:

Chapter 1 – This is an edited, reformatted and augmented version of a Congessional Research Service, Report R41120, dated April 5, 2010.

Chapter 2 – These remarks were delivered as testimony given on May 20, 2008. Senator Dick Durbin, Chairman, Subcommittee on Human Rights and the Law Hearing on "Global Internet Freedom: Corporate Responsibility and the Rule of Law".

Chapter 3 - These remarks were delivered as testimony given on May 20, 2008. Senator Tom Coburn, M.D., Subcommitte on Human Rights and the Law, United States Senate Committee on the Judiciary.

Chapter 4 - These remarks were delivered as testimony given on May 20, 2008. Nicole Wong, Deputy General Counsel, Google Inc., United States Senate Judiciary Committee Subcommittee on Human Rights and the Law.

Chapter 5 - These remarks were delivered as testimony given on May 20, 2008. Michael Samway, Vice President and Deputy General Counsel for Yahoo! Inc. before Senate Judiciary Committee Subcommittee on Human Rights and the Law.

Chapter 6 - These remarks were delivered as testimony given on May 20, 2008. Arvind Ganesan, Director, Business and Human Rights Program, Human Rights Watch to the Senate Committee on the Judiciary Subcommittee on Human Rights and the Law.

Chapter 7 - These remarks were delivered as testimony given on May 20, 2008. Mark Chandler, Senior Vice President Legal Services, General

Counsel and Secretary, Cisco Systems, Inc. before United States Senate, Committee on Judiciary Subcommittee on Human Rights and the Law.

Chapter 8 - These remarks were delivered as testimony given on May 20, 2008. Shiyu Zhou, Ph.D., Deputy Director, Global Internet Freedom Consortium before Senate Committee on the Judiciary Subcommittee on Human Rights and the Law.

Chapter 9 - These remarks were delivered as testimony given on March 24, 2010. Alan Davidson, Director of Public Policy, Google Inc. before the Congressional-Executive Commission on China Hearing on "Google and Internet Control in China: A Nexus Between Human Rights and Trade?"

Chapter 10 - These remarks were delivered as testimony given on March 24, 2010. Christine N. Jones, Executive Vice-President, General Counsel, and Corporate Secretary, The Go Daddy Group, Inc. before the Congressional-Executive Commission on China.

Chapter 11 - These remarks were delivered as testimony given on March 24, 2010. Sharon Hom, Executive Director, Human Rights in China before the Congressional-Executive Commission on China.

Chapter 12 - These remarks were delivered as testimony given on March 24, 2010. Ed Black, President and CEO, Computer and Communications Industry Association before the Congressional-Executive Commission on China.

Chapter 13 - These remarks were delivered as testimony given on March 24, 2010. Ambassador Mark Palmer, before the Congressional-Executive Commission on China.

Chapter 14 - These remarks were delivered as testimony given on March 24, 2010. Rebecca MacKinnon, Visiting Fellow, Center for Information Technology Policy, Princeton University before the Congressional-Executive Commission on China.

INDEX

A

B

C

D

G

H

I

J

L

M

N

O

P

Q

R

S

T

U

V

W

X